Better Homes and Gardens®

decks

Meredith® Books
Des Moines, Iowa

Better Homes and Gardens® Decks
Editors: Vicki Christian, Paula Marshall
Project Manager/Writer: Catherine M. Staub, Lexicon Consulting, Inc.
Contributing Editor/Writer: Julie Collins, Lexicon Consulting, Inc.
Graphic Designer: David Jordan, Studio 22
Copy Chief: Terri Fredrickson
Publishing Operations Manager: Karen Schirm
Senior Editor, Asset and Information Manager: Phillip Morgan
Edit and Design Production Coordinator: Mary Lee Gavin
Editorial Assistant: Kaye Chabot
Book Production Managers: Pam Kvitne, Marjorie J. Schenkelberg, Rick von Holdt, Mark Weaver
Contributing Copy Editor: Ira Lacher
Contributing Proofreaders: Monica Bruno, Sue Fetters, David Krause
Cover Photographer: Rob Cardillo
Indexer: Jana Finnegan

Meredith® Books
Executive Director, Editorial: Gregory H. Kayko
Executive Director, Design: Matt Strelecki
Managing Editor: Amy Tincher-Durik
Exec. Editor/Group Manager: Denise L. Caringer
Marketing Product Manager: Tyler Woods

Publisher and Editor in Chief: James D. Blume
Editorial Director: Linda Raglan Cunningham
Executive Director, New Business Development: Todd M. Davis
Executive Director, Sales: Ken Zagor
Director, Operations: George A. Susral
Director, Production: Douglas M. Johnston
Director, Marketing: Amy Nichols
Business Director: Jim Leonard

Vice President and General Manager: Douglas J. Guendel

Better Homes and Gardens® Magazine
Editor in Chief: Karol DeWulf Nickell
Deputy Editor, Home Design: Oma Blaise Ford

Meredith Publishing Group
President: Jack Griffin
Executive Vice President: Bob Mate

Meredith Corporation
Chairman and Chief Executive Officer: William T. Kerr
President and Chief Operating Officer: Stephen M. Lacy

In Memoriam: E.T. Meredith III (1933-2003)

contents

1

explore the options

Whether you work with a design professional or create the look yourself, rely on your own imagination to get the deck you want. »

>> Planning a deck begins with imagining everything you want the space to be. Even if your ideas seem far-fetched, don't discard them. Who knows? A design professional might make them a reality. Use ideas from these professional architects, landscape architects, and landscape designers to inspire your own satisfying outdoor living spaces and bring your dreams to life.

assess your needs

The beginning of this chapter taps the considerable professional experience of Bruce Pierce, landscape designer, Des Moines; Dave Rolston, landscape architect, Dallas; Sarah Nettleton, AIA, Minneapolis; Linda Searl, FAIA, Chicago; Gene Kunit, landscape architect, Sebastopol, California; Matt Moynihan, landscape architect, St. Louis; Katherine Evans, landscape architect, Alameda, California.

Many factors will influence the design of your deck. These can include the architectural style of your house, contours of your property, restrictions imposed by setbacks and codes, and location of major landscaping features, such as large trees and outbuildings. In basic terms a single-level, ranch-style house would probably look best with a low, platform-style deck. Such a plain deck would look out of place on a larger, more elaborate home. There a multilevel deck with interesting overheads—such as a pergola or an arbor—would help keep the design in proportion.

Before settling on a design, visualize how you want and perhaps need to use your new deck. Establishing clear goals for how you expect the new outdoor living space to function is key to its success.

Set primary goals by determining how your family wants to use the deck and yard. The more precise the goals, the more likely the final deck design will meet expectations. If you plan to grill most nights of the week during spring, summer, and fall, for example, an outdoor kitchen might be a requirement. If you need a comfortable, shaded spot to supervise children's outdoor play, an overhead structure becomes an essential deck accessory.

Whatever your needs, balance them against the budgetary bottom line. Later in this book you'll get a financial picture of several deck design and size options. For now just remember to keep your form and function planning in touch with your financial realities.

LEFT: A dining area makes sense if you often eat and entertain outside. A few steps from the table, a built-in granite-top island (covered by a tablecloth) makes buffet-style serving easy. Built-in benches provide extra seating and waterproof storage.

OPPOSITE: This thoughtfully composed deck and patio combination features room for a pergola, hot tub, and two conversation areas. Generous garden plantings help harmonize the various elements.

assess your feelings

Outdoor living spaces are about more than meeting needs. Decks are basically nonessential, yet delightful, areas. Planning a deck gives you freedom to assess how you want to feel when enjoying your new outdoor space. Rather than ignoring your feelings for the more practical, landscape architect Gene Kunit recommends assessing your feelings and dreams to create an ideal deck design.

"Try approaching a project with a poetic heart: Why do you want to be outside? For more intimacy? For a change of pace? How do you want to feel when you're out there? Work through these bigger questions first, then move to the details.

"Some people want to re-create the dreamy feeling of swinging on the porch at grandpa's; others want the noisy stimulation of a Parisian sidewalk cafe. To get what you really want, materials and construction have to follow the sensations and functions that you're after.

"American culture is a mix of many influences, so you can take from them all and make the space that you want. We're not locked into a singular national style, as the Japanese or English are. For an 'anything goes' country—you've got it here," Kunit says.

OPPOSITE: **Create a beautiful sense of privacy. Here a trellis and arbor built to provide privacy also support bloom-laden climbing roses in this sheltered seating area. Chaise longues offer places to read amid the terra-cotta pots and built-in planter boxes.**

ABOVE: **A cushioned swing beneath a gazebo is the perfect perch for enjoying a shady woodland paradise.**

Deck designs are no longer basic rectangles attached to the back of the house. Today's best decks integrate almost seamlessly with the house, landscape, and yard.

Landscape architect Dave Rolston recommends that you consider the entire landscape as you plan. "Try to think of the whole space, not just the deck details, but also the trees and gardens that will be part of the scene. I like to mix soft, casual plantings, such as ornamental grasses and artemisia, with more formally laid-out spaces."

As with interior design, a focal point is important for pulling a deck plan together. "Work toward organizing your design around a focal point, a philosophy, maybe a pool or a fireplace," Rolston says. "If you love birds, you can arrange a space around a birdbath. You also can work with a style—say, modernism or a Mediterranean look. Just try

to find a physical element or a theme that you can latch onto and work with to make the design special. Go to your interests for a theme. What moves you— is it travel, gardening, or art? Let that drive the design of your outdoor space. Style trends will come and go, but if your space is designed with your passions in mind, it will be timeless. And if someone respects it later, it's still timeless."

Visually connecting the deck to the architecture of your home is another strategy. Architect Linda Searl, FAIA, recommends this approach for lending style and harmonizing the deck with your home. "Railings, planters, trellises, and benches—the details of these elements can repeat and relate to those of the house," Searl suggests. "The architecture of a house can offer many clues. Check rooflines and windowpanes for shapes and themes; scout architec-

tural detailing, even fireplace surrounds."

Look to regional styles for inspiration as well. "You'll find design clues in the landscape where you live," landscape architect Gene Kunit says. "Every region has its own palette of colors and textures, so take a walk or a drive. The landscape will tell you what goes together."

ABOVE: **Under the eaves of an upper-balcony deck, this outdoor living room is protected from the elements. Wrought-iron gates are decorative and open. Stylish outdoor furniture and tropical plants complete the garden oasis in an urban setting.**

OPPOSITE: **A multilevel deck offers options for relaxing, entertaining, and gardening. Outdoor platforms linked by stairs provide ample spaces for incorporating the surrounding landscape.**

site to behold

Creating a beautiful outdoor space doesn't require a view of the mountains or sea. Sometimes finding the ideal location means thinking creatively. Landscape architect Katherine Evans says:

"Sometimes the only and best location for a deck is off the back of the house. There's nothing wrong with a single rectangle; done well, it can be quite elegant," Evans says. "But for placement, try wandering your property to find the spots that you enjoy. Go upstairs, look out the windows, and check out the rooftops, too. Then you can make notes about what you might like to do—get away for some reading here, gather with friends under the tree over there—and the design and placements will come together more easily."

If space is tight, don't forgo plans for a deck. Again, creative thinking can be key. "In Chicago, where space is tight but people want to be outdoors, we'll use whatever usable space we can find," says architect Linda Searl, FAIA. "We've designed beautiful rooftop decks, and even a deck on top of a detached garage!"

OPPOSITE: **A basic freestanding deck tucked among lush landscaping provides spectacular water views and the perfect perch for enjoying a meal.**

BELOW: **Nestled into the surrounding gardens, a rooftop deck and hops-covered pergola create the feel of Italy in summer.**

material choices

As with most consumer goods, the choices for deck materials continue to increase. While the plethora of options might prolong the planning process, you have a better opportunity to use materials that enhance or complement the look and style of your home and existing landscape. In addition, newer deck products may provide more resilient components, as landscape architect Matt Moynihan notes.

"Tropical hardwoods such as paulope have always been available, but there's been a big increase in their use for decking," Moynihan says. "These woods are exceptionally dense, rot- and bug-resistant, and are beautiful and long-lasting. The look is like that of a boat: very high quality."

Advancements in manufactured materials provide more nontraditional, yet stylish, options. Lanscape architect Gene Kunit notes: "Of course, I like to use natural materials. But I see a revolution in

progress, with steel and plastics replacing wood for increasingly attractive building material options. It's a good way to go, and it's ecologically responsible."

MAKING CONSCIENTIOUS CHOICES

Additional material options also mean you can incorporate concern for the environment into your design plans, as architect Sarah Nettleton, AIA, explains.

"Sustainable design is an important part of my design work," Nettleton says, "and is increasingly important to homeowners. How do we build what we're after without using more resources than necessary? You can start working responsibly when you tear off an existing project: Can framing material or other boards be reused? Send defective wood to the chipper. If you have hunks of concrete to haul away, call a demolition company to pick it up and grind it into road fill. You might have to make a few

phone calls to get this done, but you'll be doing something important—you'll be a hero!"

When you're ready to build the new deck, Nettleton offers these suggestions: "For your new structure, consider fabricated woods that weather just like real wood and are less likely to rot. Or ask better lumber suppliers about the availability of reclaimed wood—fine quality wood that's been stripped from buildings and structures. Finally, ask for hardwoods raised in certified sustainable forests rather than clear-cut forests. Sustainable forests—those in which trees are cut selectively rather than all at once—have even been proved to be more productive in the long run than clear-cut forests, and the big lumber companies are starting to catch on. The availability of these materials is increasing, so ask for it."

OPPOSITE: The rich characteristics of ipe—a strong, durable wood known for its furniturelike quality—makes it an eye-catching addition to any outdoor space, particularly when paired with a gazebo.

ABOVE LEFT: Low-maintenance composite decking made from synthetic material and recycled wood makes a durable surface. A lattice offers privacy and views, while the arbor serves as an open-air ceiling. A built-in corner bench provides storage and seating.

ABOVE RIGHT: Concrete dyed to blend with the brick fireplace makes fashionable, durable decking. Slatted cedar decking affords a more comfortable surface around the spa. In keeping with the home's Craftsman style, the overhead pergola is cedar as well.

details

It's all in the details. The popular saying is just as true for a successful deck as for an interior room. Consider structural details you should incorporate in your deck design during the planning process. "For the most part, the opportunity to personalize a space is in the details—the railings, benches, and planters," landscape designer Bruce Pierce notes. "Material choices are especially vast for railings and trellises—you can combine wood or iron, pipe, plexiglass, cattle fencing, even corrugated drainpipe."

The right details affect both function and form, according to landscape architect Katherine Evans. "Detail, scale, and proportion are what will distinguish a project more than anything else," she says. "For instance, if you choose a broad series of shallow, deep steps rather than the typical steep and narrow variety, your deck or terrace will have a more gracious, easy feel to it. In many cases you'll eliminate the need for guardrails too. What a boon—think about it. These rails often block your view when you're sitting down. And yet another broad step advantage: They boost your party seating capacity in a big way. Take that idea further: If there's an edge, sit on it!"

OPPOSITE BOTTOM: Plant life cascades from boxes and rises along trellises, creating a vivid, growing garden in a courtyard that offers a taste of old-world style.

ABOVE: This 800-square-foot deck offers room to dine, entertain, soak, and relax. Modern arbors add architectural interest, provide shade, and define seating areas. The slightly raised position of the deck allows expansive views.

LEFT: A graceful pergola, supported by classical columns and stone details, defines a small deck. A chandelier hanging from the pergola furthers the feeling of dining in an intimate indoor space, as do the mirror and plate racks decorating the walls.

part of a whole

ABOVE: **The juts and angles of this cedar deck blend with the angular architecture of a Swiss chalet-style house.**

RIGHT: **With French doors that lead from the kitchen to the back deck, this late-Victorian home provides easy access for relaxing. Wide, gracious steps give way to a garden shaded with mature trees.**

Creating a deck that successfully integrates with your home and landscape rather than an ill-planned afterthought will add to your enjoyment of the space.

"As you plan your outdoor space, consider its impact on the rest of your home," landscape designer Bruce Pierce says. "If the door to the deck is off the eating area, your eating area will soon become a hallway. You might want to make some indoor adjustments to accommodate this. By the same token, attached decks can block light from flowing into basement rooms. Maybe you don't care; if you do, you can build a

beautiful design that pushes the structure away from the house and still allows shafts of light through it."

Pierce offers further considerations: "Decks built over basement walkout rooms can look severe and also can cut off the sun that's needed for patio plantings below. See if you can make things more interesting and grab more light by working angles into the picture. If you're building a retaining wall,

can it come into the picture by way of a curve or an angle?

"On an even more detailed note, remember storage. If you're going to keep a water garden out there, where will you keep your tools? Nifty storage areas can be tucked into corners, railings, and under decks," Pierce suggests.

How the deck integrates with other outdoor areas is just as critical as its relation to the house. Depending on how

you plan to use the space, landscape architect Matt Moynihan suggests building a series of decks and outdoor spaces. "Families want to use their whole yards for many different purposes. It's hard for one space to have 20 different personalities. Lots of people want a place to entertain outdoors, but also a place to blow off steam or listen to music, a place to talk with a friend, and another place to feel secluded and quiet. You can get what you want, even on a small lot, by floating a series of spaces away from the house. These might be decks, patios, or a combination," Moynihan says.

Plan ahead to link the areas into a cohesive whole. "Link them with paths or steps to create a sense of open flow, and blend them with swaths of plantings to soften and naturalize the effect," Moynihan suggests. "These spaces don't need to be large or grand—people often forget to create smaller scale, intimate spaces—but these are often the spaces they value the most in the end."

ABOVE: **The exposed rafter ends and wide roof overhangs of the cedar porch and balcony contribute to the home's Arts and Crafts emphasis. Plenty of unobstructed windows provide continuous views.**

evaluate your property

The shape and prominent features of your property can give character to the design of your deck project.

Decks and their surrounding spaces are outdoor rooms, with many of the components of traditional indoor living spaces—floors, furnishings, accessories, and sometimes even walls and ceilings. Despite these similarities, the shape, contours, and physical characteristics of your property are some of the most influential elements of your deck design. Creating an outdoor living area that integrates the best attributes of your property—and avoids the worst—should be your primary goal.

As you begin to plan, take the time to get to know your property. Take photographs at different times of the day. Walk into your yard and survey areas for sun and shade. Check out the views, how close the neighbors are, and how traffic patterns lead to and from gardens, gates, and ancillary structures. Take notes about what works best and what doesn't. For example, you might notice that there is plenty of shade at the southwest corner of your property from 4 p.m. through the remainder of the evening—ideal conditions for summer entertaining. "Roughing in" the location of your deck by "seeing" where it will be is an important first step toward an effective plan.

RIGHT: **A two-level deck steps down to a seating and dining area, with lushly landscaped "rooms" beyond.**

PROPERTY CONSIDERATIONS

Four major physical characteristics affect the placement and configuration of a deck: shape, slope, shade, and views. Prominent landscaping features, such as large rocks, big trees, and gardens, also play key roles in determining how your deck will be situated. Begin by creating a map of your property that identifies important physical characteristics. See page 27 for information regarding the development of a site map. Once your map is complete, you can use it to help determine the location of your deck. See page 30, "Ideas on Paper," to learn how to sketch deck ideas.

PROPERTY SHAPE

If your property is large, there are probably many possible locations for a deck. You might have a choice between morning or evening sun, views to the south or east, and other considerations. If your house is on a modest suburban property or a smaller, narrow urban lot, however, your options are limited, and you'll need to plan space carefully. To begin planning start with a *plat* of your property: a map that shows your lot in relation to neighboring lots. It is available at your local planning and zoning office, usually free of charge. The plat shows the size and shape of your lot, and it indicates the location of any easements. These are corridors established on your property that, by law, must be kept free of any structures or impediments. Following are four examples of easements.

Utility easements provide space so crews can access electrical power lines or other utilities to make repairs. Utility easements are often at the rear of property lines, and they can run the length of the neighborhood. They are usually 5 to 10 feet wide.

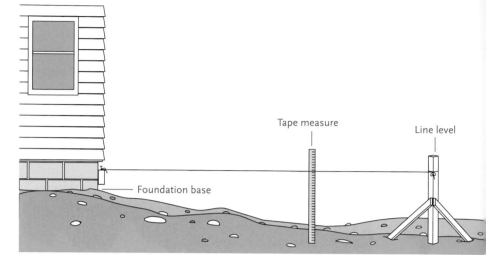

RIGHT: **Use a line and a line level to determine the amount of slope where you plan to build a deck. Measure down from the level string at regular intervals, and record your measurements.**

Overland flowage easements include significant depressions or gullies that collect running water during downpours or when snow melts. These physical land characteristics must not be altered or blocked by construction. Flowage easements prohibit structures from being built close to runoff areas where foundations could be undermined or damaged.

Accessibility easements ensure that a piece of property has direct access to a main road or byway. Creating these easements is a common practice when property is split into two parcels, creating a front-facing lot adjacent to a road, and a rear-facing lot that is not. An accessibility easement usually allows enough space for a driveway to access the main road from the rear property.

Buffer easements are created when a piece of property is next to a public park. The buffer prevents residential construction from intruding too closely on the park.

In addition to easements, construction is subject to setbacks—distances measured from the edges of a piece of property. A typical suburban lot might have a front setback of 30 to 40 feet, side setbacks of 15 feet, and rear setbacks of 10 to 20 feet. New construction cannot take place in a setback.

You can use your plat to begin making your property map and, eventually, your project. (See Chapter 2, "Plan With Purpose.") Copy your plat by hand or with a photocopier, and keep several copies to create variations of your design plans.

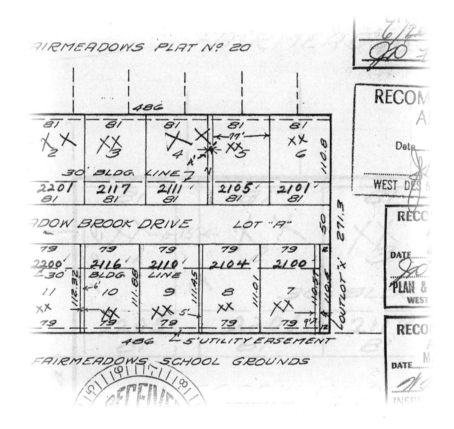

ABOVE: **A typical plat map shows the location of your house and those of your immediate neighbors. Dashed lines indicate setbacks and easements. The additional lines on this map show that annexations—subtracting a strip of land from one lot and adding it to an adjacent property—have occurred routinely.**

slope

The contours of your property—how it rises and falls—are often summed up as "slope." The slope of your property determines whether you'll need excavation and grading work or a drainage system to carry runoff away from your foundation. Decks are often less affected by slope than other structures, such as patios, because they can be built to vault over the changes in terrain. In fact, a deck is an ideal way to address a slope that may otherwise render your yard unusable. A series of tiered decks, for example, can be designed to step up a sloped lot, creating platforms. Consider designating each platform for a different use. Outfit the one nearest the house with a grill and table for outdoor dining. A middle platform with built-in benches can accommodate guests for outdoor gatherings, and a more remote, small, highest-tiered platform would be ideal as an intimate getaway spot.

Despite the flexibility of deck design, any noticeable slope may be a primary consideration when designing your project. For a vaulted deck, for instance, slope will impact the placement and size of footings and posts.

To help visualize the slope, sketch your property as seen from the side. Side views are called elevations. Your elevation should indicate the location of your house and how the surrounding property rises and falls. Take some simple measurements so you can draw your elevations as close as possible to scale.

Without using specialized equipment, such as a transit, your elevations will estimate the slope. Although not accurate, these sketches are valuable planning tools. They also are an important way to help communicate your ideas to an architect, builder, or other professional involved in the construction of your project.

To create elevations for property that falls away from the house, stretch a string line from the base of your foundation to about 20 feet. (Two people make this task easier.) Use a line level to make sure the string is plane. Measure from the string to the ground every 5 feet and record your findings on a sketch. If necessary, measure out another 20 feet, holding the string at the ground and extending it from the end of your previous measurement.

To create elevations for property that slopes toward a house, reverse the process. Begin up the slope 20 feet away from the house, then pull the string to the house and establish a level line.

ABOVE: Multiple decks can turn the slope of your backyard terrain into a delightful outdoor living space. These small decks of varying sizes and shapes link together to add interest to an otherwise uneven landscape.

Know the Code:
In many areas building codes govern allowable slope and drainage near structures. These codes are expressed as formulas. When a slope drains toward a structure, the formula might read, "Footing to toe = H/2, but need not exceed 15 feet." This means that the distance from the base of the foundation—the footing—to the base of the slope—the toe—must equal at least the height (H) of the slope divided by 2. For example, the toe of a slope 10 feet high must not be closer than 5 feet to the foundation of a house to provide adequate room for drainage. The maximum distance for any slope is usually 15 feet. Employees in your local building department can help you understand local codes.

Building codes also cover the construction of retaining walls. A retaining wall usually must be set back from a property line 1 foot for every 1 foot of height. Retaining walls higher than 3 feet need to be designed by a structural engineer.

shade

Shade changes throughout the day as the sun moves across the sky. The location of shade also changes over the course of a year. Decks are usually placed in areas where afternoon shade is available during the hottest months—on the east side of houses or under large trees. Having a deck that wraps around two or more sides of your house provides the flexibility of moving in and out of sunny or shaded areas.

If the configuration of your property does not allow you to use natural shade patterns, you might want to plan for shade structures that offer relief from the sun. (See pages 88-89, "Privacy Screens," and pages 90-93, "Overheads.") Remember that shade structures do not necessarily provide shade directly underneath. Later in the day, when the sun begins to set but still provides heat, the shade provided by an arbor or a pergola will be cast farther to the east. If you will use your outdoor deck primarily in the evening hours, plan your shade structure with that in mind, or consider adding a vertical shade screen that blocks low-angle summer sunlight.

OPPOSITE: **An overhead structure, such as this pergola, helps cast shadows late in the day, providing a shady spot for early evening dining.**

BELOW: **A wall-mounted umbrella gives flexibility in shielding guests from intense sun or rain. The wood lattice, which lets light and air filter into the space, doubles as a privacy screen.**

views

If you have great views looking outward from your home, orient your deck project to take advantage of them, even compromising certain design principles if necessary to enjoy your views. For instance, you might be willing to expose your deck to harsh western sun to be able to watch sunsets over the ocean. Or you might decide to build an expansive two-story deck on a steep lot so that you can face mountain vistas.

Negative views also are important considerations. You aren't likely to enjoy relaxing on your deck if the only view is a close up of the neighbor's garage and garbage cans, even if the light is ideal on

that side. In that case consider a new position for the deck, or plan screening to obstruct unpleasant sights.

As you make planning sketches, show the direction of the views from your property. In some instances, trees may obscure the best views. If scenery is important consider selectively cutting trees to create interesting lines of sight. If you are unsure about taking down trees, consult a landscape architect or designer so you won't destroy rare or important members of your landscape.

Don't forget to consider other views. What will passersby and neighbors see of your deck? You'll want railings, steps,

benches, overhead structures, furniture, and the surrounding landscaping to look good from every angle. And if you enjoy a particularly nice view from inside your home, be sure your deck doesn't obstruct the views from your windows.

BELOW: A panoramic setting spreads far below this flagstone terracelike deck, which has a foundation of raised concrete. Mahogany benches combine safety and seating without sacrificing spectacular views.

developing
a site map

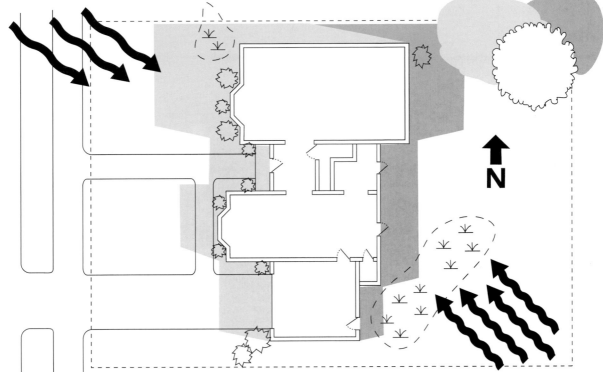

It may seem tedious at the time, but careful planning ensures that you'll build the deck you've always dreamed of. Good deck plans start with a site map, which is a scaled drawing of your property. If you've already located a plat map, you're ready to do a site analysis. If you can't find a plat map, however, you'll have to do some work.

Enlist a family member or neighbor's help to measure your yard using a 100-foot steel tape measure. Mark the locations and dimensions of the following on a sketch pad as you go along:

• Your property and property lines

• The house in relation to property lines

• Anything that may protrude from the side of the house where you plan to locate the deck, including electrical outlets, dryer vents, and water supply

• All exterior doors and windows

• Outbuildings, including garages and storage sheds, and any other major landscape features, such as large trees

and planting beds. For trees draw in the approximate trunk diameter, then lightly indicate the outer edges of the foliage.

• Roof overhangs and downspouts

• Walls, fences, stairs, sidewalks, and driveways

After examining the elements of your landscape, tape a piece of tracing paper over your site plan and trace the major elements of the site. Transfer any notes and sketches you made to the tracing paper. (Keep the original site plan intact in case you need it later.)

To complete the site analysis, analyze the conditions of your yard.

First note which direction is north. Note the prevailing winds, where the shade falls, where the sun is strongest during the time you plan to use your deck the most, and where you may need to shield your views or the views of your neighbors for extra privacy.

ABOVE: **Besides including the house in a site plan, be sure to note landscape features such as trees, shrubs, and gardens. Also indicate wind patterns, shade, and good and bad views.**

How to Measure: To accurately locate your house on a map, measure the property lines and then measure from each corner of the house perpendicular to the nearest property line.

Locate other structures, such as a tree or a patio, by measuring the distance between them and two fixed points. For example, measure the distance of a tree from two corners of the house.

Rather than trying to commit any measurements to memory, immediately write down each measurement.

plan with purpose

Establishing clear goals is the key to success. Careful planning will help ensure that your deck fulfills your expectations. »

2

>> Thorough planning means setting clear goals, establishing a budget, being familiar with the construction process, and making informed decisions that keep the project running smoothly. Determine how you'll use your deck and how elaborate the finished product will be. Consider hiring a professional architect or designer to guarantee that your vision becomes reality.

ideas on paper

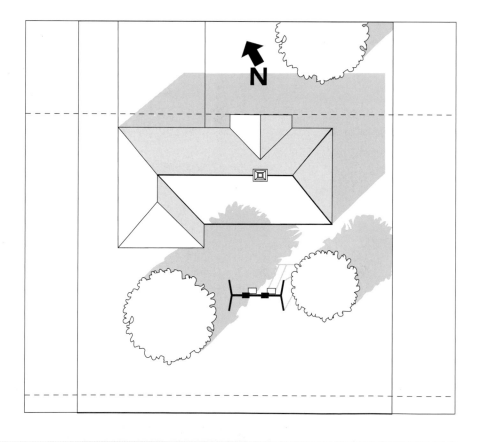

Computer-Aided Design: Landscaping software is especially useful. Many applications have a variety of ready-made symbols and graphic images of plants and small structures that you can easily place and edit. Quality landscape design programs sell at computer and electronics stores for $35 to $75.

Now that you have a site map, you're ready to begin the fun—capturing your dream deck on paper. (If you haven't developed a site map yet, see page 27.)

Tape tracing paper over your site map. Begin planning by sketching various shapes and positions for the new deck. Now is the time to experiment. If you have a grove of shade trees at the back of your property, try a platform deck detached from the house and nestled near the trees to take advantage of the shade. Consider a wraparound deck to create a small private area on one side—perhaps accessed from the master bedroom—and larger space for gatherings around the corner.

The sketches record your thoughts, work out the scale and proportion of design ideas, and visualize details. The most important reason for sketches is to communicate your ideas to architects, builders, and other professionals who are part of your project team.

There's no need to create perfect drawings. It's important that the sketches make sure all design considerations—such as traffic patterns and the location of significant landscape features—integrate into the final plan. Keep all your sketches so you can see how your design evolves.

Sketches showing a view from above are called *plan views* (*opposite*). Plan views account for the arrangement of space, clearances between furnishings, traffic patterns, and the relationship of a deck or patio to the surrounding yard and environment. Elevations give a sense of scale and help refine the design of vertical elements such as railings and privacy fences.

Once you have some sketches of decks you like, make a list of all the amenities and furnishings you want to include. Photocopy your sketches, or add another piece of tracing paper

on top of your sketch. Draw in tables, chairs, a hammock, an outdoor kitchen—whatever you plan to include. Your goal is to ensure that your sketch will become a favorite outdoor destination because it functions as you need and want.

At this point photocopy all your sketches and basic map. If you change your plans or want to compare different ideas, you easily can start fresh with a new basic map.

ABOVE: **Planning for specific uses resulted in an outdoor room made for grabbing a nap in the hammock. Wood decking and a rustic fence define an outdoor room.**

OPPOSITE: **Shade plays an important role in determining deck location. Shade in late afternoon and evening are especially important because that is usually when it's time to relax. A plan view shows patterns of shade in late afternoon. Placed where it will receive evening shade, the deck is angled to fit around a nearby maple. The design moves the swing set into a side yard visible from the deck.**

function and use

Deciding how you'll use your deck involves examining your lifestyle. Does your active family constantly occupy the backyard? Or are you just looking for a peaceful spot to relax with a morning coffee? Will you throw large, festive parties, or intimate family gatherings?

For a quiet getaway you may be content building in a small unused side yard. Strategically placed plants or a screen enhance privacy. If you entertain consider how many guests you'll invite and how much seating you'll need. Make certain you have easy access to the kitchen or an outdoor cooking area—a fully equipped outdoor kitchen ensures that you won't miss a minute of the excitement and makes serving food and drinks easier.

Perhaps the answer lies in creating multiple areas to accommodate your needs. Different levels and spaces give your design flexibility. For a small group you can confine your activities to one portion or level of your deck. If you expect larger gatherings, you can expand to other areas.

You don't need a large deck to achieve flexibility. Planters, furnishings, or overhead structures, such as pergolas or arbors, can create and define components of your overall living area. A deck with multiple levels or one that wraps around more than one side of the house ensures space for every use.

As you plan keep in mind which conveniences would be appropriate. Electrical outlets, for example, would make it easy to add or move pole and table lamps, hook up a stereo, or plug in a laptop computer.

Ultimately, before building, remember to think of your deck as an outdoor room. Figure out what you need to transform your deck into the ideal outdoor space, and you'll be well on your way to making your dream deck a reality.

OPPOSITE: A multilevel deck with an outdoor kitchen adjacent to the stairs features areas for cooking, dining, relaxing, and playing.

ABOVE: A tiered deck extending into the backyard provides an expansive outdoor living space. The large tree in the middle didn't deter the homeowners' original plans; they curved the deck around it.

landscaping design

Decks are transitional spaces that blend indoor rooms with outside environments. Significant landscaping features, such as trees and existing gardens, should be integrated carefully into your plans. When you're planning remember these key points:

• **Trees are major features** of well-planned outdoor rooms. They provide shade, privacy, and natural focal points. Make every effort to incorporate existing trees into your design. You could add trees, but the cost of installing a tree

trumpet vines and clematis, offer shade and sprays of beautiful flowers throughout the warmest months.

• **Foundation plantings** can be important additions, especially if you have a raised deck. Sturdy foundation plantings grow 2 to 4 feet high and help disguise footings, posts, and other structural components. When choosing foundation plantings, consider the amount of sunlight that will be available for your plants after the project is complete. Certain portions of your deck or

complies with codes, consult an architect or a registered structural engineer.

Moving a favorite tree out of the way is an option. For $100 to $200, trees up to 6 inches in diameter can be transplanted by a tree service that has a truck-mounted tree spade. Look in your telephone directory under "Tree Service" and "Landscape Contractors." For more information specific to your locality and type of tree, contact an arborist at your state university's agricultural department or call your state's department of agriculture or county extension service—they may provide free advice.

DESIGN PROFESSIONALS

For a fee you can contract the services of a design professional who specializes in landscaping (see "Design Professionals" on page 41). A professional makes a map of your property, integrates your project ideas, and produces a plan as extensive as you'd like. Some landscape contractors combine design and installation services.

For more information about landscaping, see page 128 ("Transitions With Landscaping").

LEFT: A tall tree built into the deck shades a bench and table. Elements of your landscape don't have to be removed to make room for decking. Contact a landscape architect for help.

OPPOSITE: Grouped together in a small grove, these oaks provide plenty of shade as they surround and grow through the middle of a deck that descends to the backyard.

large enough to provide shade—one with a trunk 3 to 6 inches in diameter—can be $500 to $1,000.

• **Large trees** might be right in the middle of your proposed deck. With a little ingenuity you can build around them. A large shade tree growing through the middle of a deck creates a delightful natural overhead shade structure.

• **Fast-growing vines** are another way to provide shade and privacy. To take advantage of a vine, you'll need to plan a trellis for the vines to climb. The trellis structure should mesh with the overall design of your deck or patio. In the right conditions a vine will grow 15 to 20 feet in a single season and provide plenty of leafy greenery by midsummer. Fast-climbing, flowering vines, such as

patio might be in full shade for most of the day, so select appropriate plants.

• **Protect existing plants** during construction. Tell your building contractor to use every caution when installing footings for a deck. A plant's root structure can be damaged during digging or by the pressure of heavy equipment moving over the ground. (Digging a few holes for foundation footings usually won't destroy a mature tree.) To prevent injury to trees, experts recommend building no closer than the tree's drip line—the outer edge of its foliage. Reduce possible root damage by designing a minimum of footings or using cantilevers that project your deck toward valuable trees and shrubs without using footings. To build a cantilever that

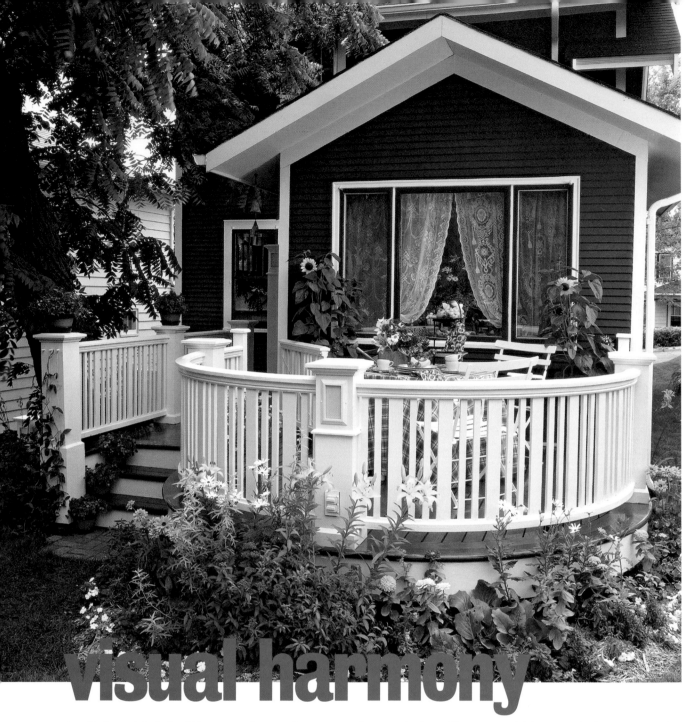

visual harmony

A well-planned deck should be a natural extension of your house, complementing its form, color, and details. Visual harmony between your deck and house is important to establish.

Not too many years ago, most decks were built with basic construction techniques and inexpensive materials—usually green pressure-treated wood. The results were sturdy, serviceable decks that had little in common with the house. Compatibility should include the size and shape of the house, the types of materials used, and the scale and placement of elements

such as stairs, railings, and arbors. The best designs integrate key features with the yard's size and existing plantings.

Although each property is unique, creating harmony follows several commonsense rules of good design.

• **Take cues from the house.** You don't have to reproduce elements precisely, but structural elements, such as posts and railings, should be thoughtfully selected and blend well with the house design. A low platform deck, for example, fits well with the shape and scale of a single-story ranch-style home. However, such a plain deck design

would be out of place attached to a larger, ornate Victorian house. For that, you would probably want to add posts and railings that complement decorative details from cornices or window trim, and possibly paint new elements to match existing woodwork.

• **Don't introduce new materials** that are radically different from what exists. A two-story brick home would look best with brick pavers for tiered landscaping and paths around the deck, rather than elaborate stonework or plain concrete. When you mix textures and colors, be sure to add elements of the original.

A turned white baluster railing bordering a redwood deck will integrate with white trim on a two-story colonial home better than contemporary wire railings.

• **Scale is important**. Don't get carried away and design a deck that threatens to overwhelm the house. Even if money is no object and you imagine the grandest of deck-patio combinations, the final design should be carefully scaled so that it is in proportion to the house.

Sketching different possibilities on paper helps you visualize changes and experiment with the deck's proportions. Even if you plan to hire a design pro, your sketches and notes are a good way to start a dialogue about which features you prefer.

BELOW: White siding, columns, railings, and accents blend with this home's custom woodworking and provide a pleasing contrast with the deck's warm tones.

OPPOSITE: A new deck can seem out of place on an older home. This one looks as if it were built along with the house, thanks to a handsome balustrade and graceful curves that reflect the home's beauty and craftsmanship.

It's exciting to imagine the ways your new deck will change your outdoor environment, but it's just as important to remember how your project will change the use of adjacent interior spaces. New doorway locations and altered traffic patterns are a few of the possible consequences of adding a deck. If your new deck is part of a more expansive renovation, make sure the traffic flows easily from one space to the other and that the changes fit your goals for comfort and livability.

Try to position the deck so it's easy to access from inside your home. You'll get more use from your deck that way. Kitchens and family rooms are good transition points for accessing a deck. These usually less formal areas are natural places for kids and pets to wander in and out of the house. Wear-resistant vinyl or tile flooring stand up to traffic well and are easy to clean.

Having a door leading from a kitchen to a deck provides easy access when entertaining. If you have a standard exterior door in this location, consider changing to a sliding patio door or a double French doorway for a larger opening and to expose interior rooms to views and light. Plan to spend $2,000 to $3,000 for a contractor to install a 6-foot-wide sliding patio door, including all materials.

As you plan sketch in traffic patterns from access doorways to deck stairs and paths. These traffic patterns should be sensible and practical. Keep tables and eating areas well away from traffic.

access and
traffic flow

If possible, place grills and cooking equipment out of the way or in special niches built just for them. Leave plenty of legroom in front of built-in benches so guests won't have to retract their legs every time someone walks past.

OPPOSITE: Two sets of doors and multiple seating areas provide ample room to move when entertaining. Stationing the grill and tables near the doors makes carrying food or dishes to and from the kitchen an easy task.

ABOVE: French doors that open from the family room onto the deck allow easy indoor-outdoor traffic flow to and from an outdoor space designed to integrate the style of a 100-year-old home.

universal design

Universal design is an approach to design—whether indoors or out—that makes living easier for people with physical challenges. By following universal design principles, you can create an outdoor space that helps accommodate wheelchairs and makes access easier for everyone.

Use under-deck brackets to attach decking boards rather than nails or screws, which could be treacherous for wheelchairs. Ensure doors leading from the house to the deck are 32 to 36 inches wide, have lever door handles, feature a no-step entry/exit, and have flush thresholds. Avoid level changes on the deck, which can make navigating in a wheelchair difficult; instead, designate areas for different uses with a change in decking pattern. Make certain there's room for a wheelchair to turn completely around—a clear space approximately 5 feet in diameter—as well as ample sitting space. Raised planters on the deck provide easy-access gardening. Ramps make it possible to access gardens, sidewalks, or other surrounding areas.

BELOW: Shallow edge guards ensure safety on the multiple gently sloping ramps. Plantings in the open areas between pathways blend with the lush plants located beyond this deck.

design
professionals

A professional designer creates a space that meets your needs. Because of their expertise and experience, professionals can offer fresh ideas, anticipate code restrictions, and deal with unusual problems. If the cost of hiring a designer seems prohibitive, consider that professionals can help save on overall costs by contributing to the efficiency of the project, organizing and managing workflow, and helping to avoid expensive mistakes. Many are willing to work for an hourly fee.

When working with a professional, good communication is key to achieving your goals. Start a clipping folder. Use it to keep articles and photographs cut from magazines that show ideas and design elements that appeal to you. Add product brochures or advertisements that you can show your designer. Draw sketches of your ideas and share them with your designer. A good designer is interested in your lifestyle and should ask questions and take notes about how you live, your daily routine, and your project goals.

Three types of design professionals can work on a deck project. Although they have specialized areas of expertise, most professionals are well-versed in all phases of design and can help create a comprehensive plan.

• **Architects** work primarily with structure and reorganization of space. They are familiar with many types of building materials, finishes, and structural systems. A good choice for complex deck designs, an architect designs your deck and makes sure it sensibly integrates with adjacent living areas, such as your kitchen or family room. Architects charge a percentage of the project's total cost, usually 10 to 15 percent, or $50 to

$125 per hour. For a listing of architects in your area, look in your phone directory. Or try the Internet search engine offered by the American Institute of Architects at: www.aia.org/architect_finder.

• **Landscape architects** registered with the American Society of Landscape Architects (ASLA) usually are designers only; the plans they furnish must be given to a landscape contractor for final installation. Occasionally a landscape architect joins with a landscape contractor to offer full-service planning and installation. An ASLA architect charges $75 to $125 per hour to inspect and analyze the property, and then complete detailed drawings. These drawings recommend plantings and landscape features that help connect the new space to the outdoor environment. To create a plan expect to pay 15 percent of the cost of the finished landscape project. To find a landscape architect, consult your telephone directory under "Landscape Architects" or check with the American Society of Landscape Architects at www.asla.org.

• **Landscape contractors** can install decks, patios, walkways, retaining walls, plantings, and ancillary structures, such as pergolas and arbors. Many landscape

contractors are full-service business firms that include landscape architects, designers, and installers. They can provide a full range of services that include initial concepts, finalized plans, installation, and maintenance. If required by state law, a landscape contracting company should be licensed or certified, indicating they have passed examinations and have demonstrated expertise and knowledge, and also that they participate in ongoing programs of education. Find "Landscape Contractors" in your telephone directory or contact the Associated Landscape Contractors of America at www.alca.org.

ABOVE: **Although the homeowners did much of the work on their raised deck themselves, they relied on experienced design professionals for a few key steps. After sketching their ideas the homeowners met with a local designer who provided a working plan. Once they set up a grid on their property, the homeowners located a contractor to dig the postholes.**

running electricity

Careful planning of your electrical needs helps ensure your satisfaction. If you plan to use your new deck as a supplemental outdoor kitchen, you might need individual circuits to run small appliances, such as cooktops and rotisseries. A few electrical outlets accommodate stereo equipment or a laptop computer. Outdoor landscape lighting also requires electrical planning, unless you select solar-powered lights.

Calculate your home's power requirements to determine if you need additional circuits to handle the increased load. A licensed electrical contractor can make these calculations and guarantee that your project conforms to specifications by the National Electrical Code (NEC). A modest deck usually can be serviced by splicing into an existing circuit. More extensive remodeling could require adding a circuit. Your design professional or general contractor should be able to estimate the cost for electrical work. If you are acting as your own general contractor, take bids from several electrical contractors to establish a price.

When splicing into an existing circuit, an electrician adds wiring to an existing junction box or adds a junction box along existing wiring. Junction boxes often are located in open attic or basement spaces, where they are readily accessible. Occasionally an electrician must open up walls and ceilings to access wiring and add new junction boxes. The expense of repairing walls and ceilings is part of the cost of the project.

Outdoor receptacles should be placed in weatherproof boxes, with spring-loaded outlet covers that seal against moisture. Also most building codes require that an outdoor receptacle be protected by a ground fault circuit interrupter (GFCI). If there is a short circuit, GFCI-type receptacles detect the deviation in current and instantly shut off power to the receptacle.

ABOVE: **Small lights built into deck stairs enable guests to see where they are stepping. Incorporating outdoor lighting into your design requires careful planning.**

plumbing

Incorporating a water element into your backyard isn't easy—whether it's a shower, spa, swimming pool, or outdoor kitchen. Plumbing for a water element makes the job more difficult, but the results are worth it. Work with a design professional to plan the location of your utilities. (Make certain your plan meets local codes.) Even if you won't add an amenity, such as an outdoor kitchen, until later in the project, rough in the utilities during site-prep work.

Control plumbing costs by situating an outdoor bath or kitchen close to a hot water line in an outside wall of your home—it's less expensive than installing new underground lines. A plumber can tap into your existing water supply and drain lines.

Running water and drain connections underground avoids clutter and prevents damage. But keep in mind that the connections must be easily accessible for maintenance.

Fountains, ponds, pools, and other water features rarely require a water supply line to feed water. However, you may wish to have a plumber run a supply line you can shut off and drain during the winter as a convenience for refilling.

Living where the ground freezes also complicates the plan for a water system. For instance, if your outdoor kitchen is detached from the house, the pipes need to run underground in a trench 12 inches below the frost line.

To construct a full supply and drain system for water, hire a plumber. If you want only a prep sink in your outdoor kitchen, however, go for a low-tech approach by supplying it with water from a garden hose. Such a sink requires only a few standard pipe fittings, such as a hose connection on the cooking center.

Place a portable reservoir for gray water (a specialized 5-gallon container) inside the cooking-center base so you can clean produce, rinse plates, or wash your hands. If you avoid using harsh cleaners or chemicals, you can empty the wastewater onto plants.

If you install a shower on or near the deck, you need a drain to catch runoff. You may have to tie into your home's sewer line. Or install a French drain—a pipe buried below ground and set in gravel.

ABOVE: **A 6-foot-tall privacy fence surrounding a hot tub doubles as an outdoor shower stall. Connect the spa's hot water supply to a basic shower line for a quick rinse.**

TOP: **A handy side table holds a stainless-steel sink and shelves. Situate a sink close to the house to tap into your home's hot water line. Or use a prep sink that may be supplied with water from a garden hose.**

outdoor lighting

A well-designed outdoor lighting system allows you to use your deck in comfort and safety during the evening. It should illuminate key points, such as conversation areas, cooking centers, doors, walkways, pool surrounds, and stairs. It also can be used to highlight special features, such as plants or trees, and can provide security lighting around foundation plantings and fences.

Outdoor lighting comes in three types: regular fixtures that use 120-volt household current, low-voltage, and solar-powered. Low-voltage lighting is increasingly popular because it is safe, inexpensive, and easy to install. Manufacturers of low-voltage lighting offer an array of styles and configurations made especially for outdoor residential use. These are readily available at home improvement centers. Low-voltage and solar lights are either freestanding units or fasten to posts, railings, stair risers, and other components.

BULB BASICS

Lamps, or bulbs, cast different kinds of light. The familiar **incandescent bulbs** are relatively inexpensive. They have a warm, natural quality of light that is especially pleasing on faces. These lights can be dimmed with rheostat switches—a real advantage for design flexibility. **Quartz-type incandescent lamps** provide a more intense, "whiter" light. **Tungsten-halogens** are low-voltage types of incandescent bulbs. Though they last longer and use less electricity than standard incandescent bulbs, they produce intense heat. **Xenon bulbs** are an alternative to halogens, without the intense heat and delicate handling requirements. They are expensive, however.

High-intensity discharge (HID) lamps include metal halide, mercury vapor, and high-pressure sodium lamps.

Planning for Lighting: When planning a lighting scheme, keep the design as flexible as possible so your lighting is appropriate for a variety of uses. Use several circuits and incorporate dimmer switches that allow you to control the amount of light in individual areas. Place switches indoors.

If you also want switches outdoors, you need to have three-way switches installed. To avoid glare make sure the light source—the bulb—is hidden from direct view by shades, covers, or plantings, or by letting light bounce off large reflective surfaces, such as walls.

An outdoor lighting system usually combines several lighting techniques. The most common types:

• *Downlighting* is placed on poles, in trees, or on the sides of houses. It shines directly onto surfaces and is used for general illumination and safety.

• *Uplighting* is placed low to the ground and directed upward for dramatic effect and to highlight individual objects, such as unusual trees or garden sculptures.

• *Passage lighting* illuminates pathways and stairs. A series of small downlights usually leads the way along a defined route.

• *Area lighting* illuminates larger surfaces, such as lawns, patios, and decks. Several types of lighting produce an overall effect that is not too harsh or distracting.

RIGHT: **Distinctive illumination makes a multilevel deck come alive at night. Small spotlights illuminate translucent planter box panels from behind, and discrete semicircle fixtures provide downlighting for the steps.**

OPPOSITE: **Theater lights set into the stairs provide enough light for climbing at night. Lighting along the roofline accentuates the gazebo's shape.**

All provide reliable, brilliant light and are especially energy-efficient, but they are not recommended for use with dimmer switches. Some people are bothered by the orange or greenish cast of HID lamps. This type of bulb is used primarily for safety lighting around pools or for illuminating large activity areas, such as tennis courts.

Fluorescent bulbs are a budget-friendly choice. This type of lamp lasts longer in fixtures that aren't turned off and on frequently. Fluorescents can cast a harsh light. For the most pleasing light, look for color-corrected or warm bulbs.

bulbs

Here's what you'll find when you go bulb shopping for outdoor lighting fixtures:

INCANDESCENT. Most commonly used bulb type. **Pros:** Casts a warm, pleasant light. Can be dimmed with rheostat switches. Least expensive. **Cons:** Produces a lot of heat. Can dim with use.

TUNGSTEN-HALOGEN. Low-voltage, pricier type of incandescent bulb that produces an intense beam. **Pros:** Ideal for accent lighting. Won't dim with age. Can last four times as long as incandescent bulbs. Uses less electricity. **Cons:** Beams can produce intense heat. Must be used away from fabrics, paper, and flammable materials. Must be handled carefully. Direct contact with skin will contaminate it, damage the glass, and cause it to burn out rapidly.

HIGH-INTENSITY DISCHARGE (HID). Includes metal halide, mercury vapor, and high-pressure sodium lamps. Used primarily for safety lighting near pools and illuminating large areas, such as tennis courts. **Pros:** Reliable, brilliant light. Energy-efficient. **Cons:** Not recommended for dimmer switches. Orange or greenish cast.

XENON. Brightness of halogen bulb without the intense heat and delicate handling. **Pros:** Low voltage. Energy-efficient. **Cons:** Expensive.

FLUORESCENT. Lasts longer in fixtures that aren't turned off and on frequently. For the most pleasing light quality, look for color-corrected or warm white bulbs. **Pros:** Budget-savvy choice. Uses just a third of the electricity and costs less over time than incandescent. **Cons:** Can cast a harsh light.

planning
the budget

A workable budget usually is a compromise between all the great things you imagine for your finished project and what you ought to budget to achieve your goals. Your first priority should be to set limits for the total amount of money you spend. Make two lists. One should include everything you consider essential for your new space. The other should be the amenities you'd like to have if money is left over. Don't add extras until costs for the essentials are finalized.

As you complete your ideas and move toward construction, request bids from contractors and other professionals. Add a 5 to 10 percent cushion to cover cost overruns and changes to plans that can occur after construction begins. Have a firm idea of what you would like to spend and tell it to all the professionals involved. A commitment to your bottom line helps you make the difficult cost-cutting decisions if your project threatens to go over budget.

Though your budget must include all the essentials, you can save money by comparison shopping and researching alternatives. Certain decking materials, for example, are more expensive than

others. Where you live also is a factor in costs. If wood is locally grown, for example, it will be less expensive than if it must be shipped across the country.

Another budget-savvy approach is to construct your deck in stages. If your final plan is a large, multilevel deck, with outdoor kitchen and gazebo, all surrounded by a flagstone patio, you could break up the project into four parts: 1) the deck; 2) the gazebo, 3) the flagstone patio; and 4) the outdoor kitchen. In the initial construction phase, rough in whatever utilities and substructures you need. Then tackle one part of the project at a time, as money permits.

You may also consider doing some of the work yourself. Be cautious and realistic about this approach. You still have expenses for all of the materials. If you don't have the tools for deck building, purchasing and renting the right equipment could add up.

RIGHT: **Even a modest-size deck requires careful budget planning, especially to account for thoughtful amenities such as the elegant overhead, stone pillars, and new access doors.**

Avoid Budget-Busters: Control costs by finalizing your deck plans before work begins. One of the biggest budget-blowers is changing your plans once work is underway. Make sure you spend plenty of time planning before leaping into construction. Changing the size of the deck on paper may result in only minimal charges if you've hired a design professional to draw your final plans. Changing the size after construction begins could result in significant expense and could even require starting the building from scratch. Even a seemingly simple change, such as decking pattern, should be made before beginning work. Different decking patterns require different framing that could mean significant expense once work is underway.

3

elements of style

Learning about the materials and methods of deck construction is the first step toward building the deck of your dreams. »

>> You have an enormous array of deck materials, finishes, and embellishments from which to select. To make certain your deck looks great and fits your lifestyle, take time to learn about the many possibilities: You'll be able to make informed decisions that will allow your project to proceed smoothly and efficiently. The result will be a deck that is a joy to use and enhances your property.

platform

Deck designs are so diverse that it's difficult to pinpoint a particular style. However, identifying four basic configurations—platform, raised and two-story, multilevel, and freestanding—is a good place to begin your design.

Platform decks are the simplest, usually built on level lots and attached to single-level dwellings. They are so low to the ground that railings often aren't necessary. (Most building codes require railings and balusters if the deck is 24 inches or more above the ground. Check local codes before proceeding.)

On gently sloped lots build a series of platforms that step down gradually to follow the contour of the land. Built-in planters and bench seating around the perimeter give substance and mass to platform decks.

Because platform decks are close to the ground, it is important that the materials are impervious to moisture. Structural materials for any deck should be pressure-treated or rated for direct ground contact. For decking and other platform deck parts, make certain all materials receive two coats of protective sealer before they are installed so the undersides are well-preserved. In humid areas install a vapor barrier of plastic sheeting before construction. Cover the vapor barrier with 2 or 3 inches of soil or gravel to conceal it.

ABOVE: A platform deck is built low to the ground and may not require railings. Built-in benches help define the deck perimeter.

OPPOSITE: Though platform decks are the most basic type, nothing beats a deck that seamlessly incorporates angles, curves, and a large screened gazebo. The sunburst railing and other details ensure that this deck has style.

raised and

Raised decks are common because most houses sit on foundation walls that position the first-level floor above grade. They require railing systems for safety and stairs to make the deck accessible to the yard. Designing good-looking railing systems and locating stairs that establish practical traffic patterns are keys to success.

Raised decks have foundation posts that are exposed when the structure is complete. The structural members can be concealed with foundation plantings or with skirting. Skirting usually consists of lath or lattice panels cut to fit between the deck surface and the ground. The cut paneling is attached to perimeter posts. This type of skirting hides the structural system yet permits air to circulate under the deck, discouraging problems associated with excessive moisture. Lattice panels also prevent large animals, such as raccoons, from taking a liking to the protected area under your deck. For more information, see pages 84-85.

Two-story decks provide outdoor access to upper-level areas of your home. The structural posts and bracing required to support a two-story deck can be quite tall and present an aesthetic challenge. Posts can be made thicker than codes require, or they can be faced with decorative boards so they won't appear spindly. Partial skirting or decorative pieces spanning exterior posts help create a balanced design.

two-story

ABOVE: For solidity and performance, this two-level deck uses 12×12 posts with angled support timbers to adequately support the second story. Bump-outs and railing details add dramatic visual interest.

OPPOSITE TOP: With a gazebo at one end and a swim spa at the other, a redwood deck transitions from house to yard.

OPPOSITE BOTTOM: Second-level decks must take into account the appearance of exposed structural members. This example uses rock-faced pillars to support the structure. The upper-level balcony supplies uninterrupted views of the spectacular canyon beyond.

Multilevel decks are a series of decks connected by stairways or walkways. They are usually designed for yards with sloped lots so that the deck areas follow the contours of the land. A tall main deck that otherwise might gain access to the surrounding yard through a long stairway can be built as a series of smaller deck spaces, each joined by a short run of stairs. This arrangement prevents the lowest deck—the one farthest from the house—from interfering with views from decks higher up.

A multilevel deck takes advantage of microclimates within your yard. Have one level close to the house for entertaining, another one in the cool shade of nearby trees, and yet another placed to take in the sun.

OPPOSITE: A multilevel, 16×12-foot deck offers shelter from the elements beneath the balcony and space on the lower level to soak up the sun.

BELOW: Working with the rugged shape of a rising hill, terraced platforms surround natural elements and provide multiple levels for conversation and dining.

freestanding

Freestanding decks are not attached to the house. These separate landscaping features usually are located some distance from the main living areas, where they can provide the best views or be positioned in a shady glade or in a beautiful garden.

Freestanding decks can be positioned next to the house. This is a useful approach when the construction of the house doesn't allow for a ledger board (see page 59). Also, if your design calls for three cascading platforms, freestanding decks would be easier than attaching ledgers at three levels.

Freestanding decks are built with the same basic methods and techniques as attached decks, except that footings, posts, and beams replace the ledger.

ABOVE: With its low profile this freestanding deck appears to be a natural extension of the bordering landscape. The structure is enhanced by a pergola and potted plants.

OPPOSITE: A basic pavilion perched atop a freestanding deck extends an Asian ambiance. Wood-grid partitions and translucent acrylic panels evoke the airy look of rice paper screens.

anatomy of a deck

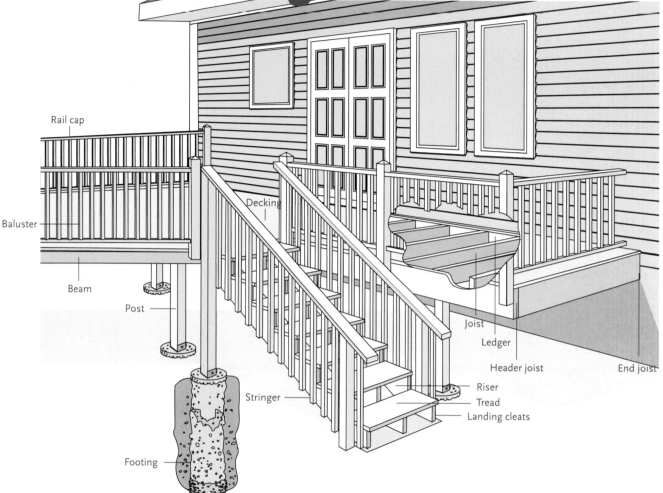

Rail cap

Baluster

Beam

Post

Footing

Decking

Stringer

Joist

Ledger

Header joist

End joist

Riser

Tread

Landing cleats

Decks are basic structures, but the final design can be complex. It's essential to become familiar with the terms used in deck construction when planning a deck, ordering materials, and overseeing any changes to plans while the deck is being built. Understanding deck terminology helps you communicate effectively with designers, builders, and other contractors. Here are some important terms:

• **Footings** are cylinders of poured concrete that extend into the ground and support individual posts. Building codes require that they extend below the frost line. This prevents the seasonal cycles of freezing and thawing from disturbing the position of the footings over the years. A footing usually is 36 to 42 inches deep. The location of the footings

depends on the size and shape of the deck.

• **Pier blocks** (not illustrated) are set on top of footings while the footing concrete is still wet. Made of precast concrete and about 8 inches on each side, they elevate the posts to keep them from coming into contact with the ground, preventing moisture damage. Some pier blocks include metal hardware for a secure connection to posts.

• **Posts** extend up from the footings and form the vertical supports of a deck. The thickness of the posts depends on the configuration of the deck structure. Thicker posts spaced farther apart can take the place of thinner posts that are closer together. Posts should be made of pressure-treated lumber to retard rot and

insect attack. Tall posts—such as those required for second-story decks—need angled supports called *bracing* to provide stability.

• **Joists** form a grid for supporting the decking material. Often called "two-by" lumber, joists are 1½ inches thick and are installed on edge. The sizes of the joists are determined by the span of the deck: the longer the span, the heftier the joist. The joists at the perimeter of a deck are called *rim joists*. Rim joists usually are doubled to provide firm support around the deck edges.

• **Beams**, or girders, are large pieces of lumber used to support joists. The beams are attached to the posts and run at right angles to the joists. Depending on the size and configuration of a deck, beams

may not be necessary. Like all structural components, beams made from pressure-treated lumber combine strength and durability.

• **Ledger board** is a joist mounted against the side of a house to provide support for one side of a deck. The ledger board is bolted or screwed to the house; the space behind the ledger is sealed with caulk and covered with flashing to prevent water from penetrating to the interior of the house. Joists usually are attached to the ledger with joist hangers—

galvanized metal holders that provide firm, secure support.

• **Fascia boards** (not illustrated) cover rim joists. They are usually 1-inch-thick boards made from a good-looking wood such as cedar or redwood and often cover joists made from pressure-treated lumber. For a clean, finished appearance, fascia may be mitered at the corners. Wood exposed to harsh outdoor climates tends to expand and contract, opening even the tightest miter joints over time.

• **Decking** covers joists and forms the main surface area. Decking usually is

installed flat and fastened with galvanized nails or screws. Decking boards are spaced 1/8 to 3/16 inches apart to provide drainage and to allow the wood to contract and expand.

ABOVE: **Customizing a basic deck transforms it into an ideal outdoor living space. Built-in benches add seating and handy serving space for year-round outdoor dining and entertaining. Cedar arbors towering over the benches provide shade.**

decking

Most of your deck is a large, flat surface—decking. Because decking is such a prominent feature, it should be attractive, durable, smooth, and free of cracks, splinters, and other defects.

Wood decking is easy to work with and comes in a range of prices. A number of synthetic products resemble wood. These products usually are more expensive than wood, but most are virtually maintenance-free.

Because decks are so popular, different types of decking materials are widely available in all areas.

WOOD DECKING

Several types of wood are used for decking, railing systems, and embellishments such as planters, pergolas, and built-in furniture. These woods have attractive grain patterns and colors. Popular deck materials include:

• **Redwood** naturally resists rot and decay. It should be treated with clear

sealers each year. A soft wood with a distinctive reddish hue, it has a tight, uniform grain pattern that is exceptionally attractive. Redwood is also an excellent paint-grade wood, although the cost of redwood would suggest it should be used in its natural state for best effect.

• **Cedar** is lightweight and naturally resists rot and decay. It has streaks of cream and brown, and occasional knots. The 1×6 cedar boards made specifically as decking material are 5½ inches wide and 1 inch thick, and have rounded

ABOVE: This 27×18-foot deck is constructed from ipe, a Brazilian hardwood known for minimal maintenance.

OPPOSITE: Mahogany's rich color and resistance to splintering makes it natural for outdoor spaces. Curving the edge of this mahogany deck was an effective use of space and a reflection of the home's contours.

Pressure-Treated Wood Safety: Pressure-treated wood decking is saturated with chromated copper arsenate (CCA) to make it resist rot and decay. It is safe to touch and handle, is not dangerous to plants, and will not leach into groundwater. Nevertheless, you should observe certain precautions when working with pressure-treated wood. Wear a dust mask when cutting it. Never burn pressure-treated wood; it could release toxins into the air. Dispose of pressure-treated scraps by placing them in the garbage.

edges that prevent splintering. Cedar decking is widely available.

• **Cypress** is lightweight and naturally resists rot and decay. A soft wood with a varied grain pattern, it is readily available in the South.

• **Pressure-treated wood** is widely used as decking. Strong and less expensive than other decking materials, it comes in green or brown, the result of chemicals that enable the wood to resist moisture, decay, and insect attacks. Some people consider the color unattractive; however, pressure-treated wood can be stained or painted. Com-

bining great strength with low cost, it is available throughout North America.

Construction-grade pressure-treated lumber often is used for the structural parts of a deck—the posts, girders, and joists. When exposed to the elements, the surface of the medium-grade fir or pine used for structural parts tends to crack and split, although it doesn't lose its strength. Because these components are usually hidden from view, the appearance of the material is not a concern.

Construction-grade pressure-treated wood should not be used for decking. Instead, be sure to specify pressure-

OPPOSITE: Western red cedar, mahogany, and pine combine in this attractive deck. Cedar and mahogany were used for the railings; the floorboards are mahogany. White-painted pine boards, installed between the floorboards and the ground, match the house's white trim.

BELOW: Durable and attractive, cedar is a natural choice for the large size and different levels of this deck. To keep the cedar looking like new for more than 15 years, the homeowners regularly clean the deck and apply a nonpetroleum-base penetrating wood finish yearly.

Expert Advice

Almost all wood turns silvery gray when exposed to the elements. To preserve the original color of woods such as cedar and redwood, you should clean it and apply clear sealer every year.

treated 1×6s that are manufactured especially for use as decking. This material is 5½ inches wide, 1 inch thick (also referred to as ⁵⁄₄ thickness), has few knots, and has rounded edges that resist splintering.

• **Ipe** is a tropical hardwood that is increasingly popular for deck construction despite being heavy, expensive, and difficult to cut and drill. Ipe boards also must be predrilled to install fasteners. However, it is impervious to the elements, resists insects, and has the same fire rating as concrete or steel. Best of all it's a beautiful, lustrous brown. Order ipe from a hardwood dealer.

• **Meranti** is another tropical hardwood. Slightly less expensive than other exotic woods, it resists decay and rot. Like ipe, it must be predrilled. Grain pattern is consistent in this light red to dark red-brown wood. Meranti weathers to a rich gray.

SYNTHETIC DECKING

Several kinds of synthetic decking materials are available as alternatives to wood. Some have wood-like textures and can be cut and fastened with the same tools and techniques used for wood. However, most are not strong enough to be used as structural members and are intended only for decking. They cost more than wood of similar sizes, but have lower maintenance requirements.

• **Plastic decking** comes in several colors and textures. It is lightweight and easy to install with a system of clips that allows the decking to expand and contract.

• **Vinyl decking** has similar properties to plastic and is available in a variety of colors. The nonslip textured surface resembles manufactured metal rather than wood. Look for brands that have

Composite Upgrades: Early composite lumber was touted to be maintenance-free. However, consumers found that composites were as susceptible to mold, mildew, staining, and fading as wood, and required maintenance. Manufacturers are looking for ways to meet the demand for lower-maintenance, better-performing composite decking. CorrectDeck, for example, recently added to some of its products an antimicrobial protectant that is designed to resist mold, mildew, staining, color fading, and slipping.

REDWOOD. Color: Pink to deep red; might have streaks of cream-color sapwood. **Strength:** Low to moderate. **Availability:** Most of the country. **Cost:** $1.50 per lineal foot of 1×6.

CEDAR. Color: Light tan to medium brown with streaks of cream. **Strength:** Low. **Availability:** Most of the country. **Cost:** 85 cents per lineal foot of 1×6.

CYPRESS. Color: Various browns. **Strength:** Medium. **Availability:** Primarily in the South. **Cost:** 65 cents per lineal foot of 1×6.

PRESSURE-TREATED PINE OR FIR. Color: Tinted green or brown. **Strength:** Medium. **Availability:** Widely. **Cost:** 45 cents per lineal foot of 1×6.

IPE. Color: Lustrous chocolate brown. **Strength:** High. **Availability:** By special order, though as it gains popularity, more readily available. **Cost:** $3.50 to $4 per lineal foot of 1×6.

MERANTI. Color: Light red to dark reddish-brown. **Strength:** High. **Availability:** By special order, though becoming more readily available. **Cost:** $3.50 to $4 per lineal foot of 1×6.

SYNTHETICS. Color: Pure white, tan, gray, various browns, and green. **Strength:** Used only for decking, not structural components. **Availability:** Usually available, though perhaps not all products at one location. **Cost:** $2 to $4 per lineal foot of 1×6.

ultraviolet (UV) light inhibitors impregnated into the material. UV inhibitors prevent fading caused by sunlight.

• **Composite lumber** is made from wood fibers mixed with resins derived from recycled plastic. This decking is the most realistic-looking of the synthetics, is easy to cut and nail, and can be stained. Look for brands made with polypropylene—it creates a stronger, stiffer board that is less likely to sag.

• **Rubber lumber** is made from a mixture of recycled plastics and recycled rubber from old tires. It comes in only a few colors, but it is tough, durable, and impervious to rot, insects, and UV light.

OPPOSITE: A deck constructed of *Trex*, a synthetic composite material made from recycled wood and plastic, requires less maintenance than wood. The surface is less prone to splintering, warping, or cracking, and it's not necessary to cover the decking with a protective coating.

LEFT: A table and adirondack chairs create an inviting refuge on a deck of concrete. The deck is paired with Craftsman-inspired elements, including a waterproof cedar pergola with handrails and a privacy fence.

decking patterns

Decking is usually installed in long strips that run parallel to the face of the house and perpendicular to joists. You can add visual interest by installing decking diagonally, or by making patterns that display creative flair. Patterned decking is one way to break up the expanse of a large deck.

Patterns should be planned to avoid partial grids or incomplete patterns at the deck's perimeter. Some patterns require additional joists or structural framing to provide enough nailing surfaces for the ends of the decking boards.

You can create interesting decking patterns only by drawing plans that show the proper framing. For illustrations of some popular patterns, see page 67.

• **Standard patterns** have the decking running perpendicular to the joists and parallel to the longest face of the house. This is the least expensive and least complicated way to install decking.

• **Diagonal decking** is usually installed at a 45-degree angle to the joists. Altering the joist pattern or adding joists usually is not necessary. But angled cuts at the ends of the decking waste wood and require 5 to 10 percent more boards than a standard pattern.

• **Parquet or grid patterns** are modular squares featuring decking boards that change directions. A common practice is to have the boards of each square run perpendicular to the adjacent squares. A variation is a geometric pattern of modular grids featuring diagonal decking.

BELOW: For greater visual impact, install your decking in an interesting pattern. A basket-weave pattern dresses up this platform deck.

LEFT: Narrow 2×4 decking intersects with a cross of 2×8s, which breaks up the surface into quadrants. The white paint of the railing and furniture enhances the inlaid floor's dark green stain.

BELOW LEFT: The bold pattern of nested squares adds drama to otherwise plain decking. Trimmed edges give the adjoining steps a finished look.

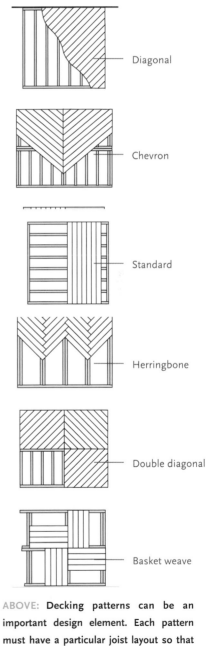

Diagonal

Chevron

Standard

Herringbone

Double diagonal

Basket weave

ABOVE: Decking patterns can be an important design element. Each pattern must have a particular joist layout so that the ends of the decking boards are adequately supported.

fasteners

Don't scrimp on the quality of fasteners when building—they hold your deck together! Screws, nails, and anchoring hardware must stand up to years of wear and are particularly vulnerable to moisture. It's best to use coated fasteners made specifically for decks.

NAILS

A nail's size is determined by its length, which is called *pennyweight* (abbreviated as "d"). Gauge, or diameter, increases as the pennyweight increases.

Common nails, used for general construction, have large heads and thick shanks. They hold well, but are hard to drive and may split the wood.

Box nails, thinner than common nails of the same size, reduce splitting in stock that is ¾ inch or thinner.

Ringshank and spiral nails grip the wood fibers better than common or box nails. Although they don't easily work their way out, they are difficult to remove.

Finishing nails have slender shanks and small, barrel-shape heads that can be countersunk. Use them for trim work and in places where you don't want the heads to show.

Casing nails are heftier versions of finishing nails, with more holding power.

When selecting nail composition, stainless steel is a costly, but smart, choice. The most common type of nails are galvanized, which should resist rust, although the coating on the nails often flakes off. Aluminum nails won't rust, but they aren't as strong as galvanized nails and can be difficult to drive into harder woods because they bend.

SCREWS

Screws hold better than nails because they don't pop out of the wood, plus they're easier to remove. They come in an astonishing array of styles, which can make selection difficult. A good all-around choice is #10 decking screws, generally in 2½- to 3½-inch lengths. Decking screws are coated for resistance to the elements and are sharp, tapered, and self-sinking. With a cordless drill you can drive them almost as fast as nails.

Match your screwdriver bit to the screw head (or vice versa). Decking screws are usually machined with a phillips, square, or combination head. Square heads drive more securely.

HEAVY-DUTY SCREWS AND BOLTS

Nails and screws are the most commonly used fasteners, but bigger connections call for heavy-duty hardware. To fasten a large post, use either a lag screw or a car-riage bolt. Bolts are stronger and can be tightened later if the lumber shrinks. Use washers under the head of a lag screw or the nut on a carriage bolt so the fastener does not sink into the wood.

Attach a ledger to brick, block, or concrete with lag screws and masonry anchors. To hold the ledger temporarily, use masonry screws, which are not quite as strong but are easier to drive and don't require anchors.

FRAMING HARDWARE

Framing connectors strengthen the joints between framing members. Most current building codes require framing hardware for joining framing members.

Attach joists to a ledger or beam using joist hangers. Where a beam sits on top of a post, a post cap provides a reliable joint. A post anchor secures a post to a concrete pier and supports it so the bottom can dry between rainfalls.

LEFT: Ask about the specific type of fastener best suited for the type of decking you'll be using. Some fasteners are designed to work with a particular type of composite, for example. Others will work with most standard deck boards.

Invisible Supports: Hidden decking supports are another option for fastening decking. Since you don't see them, they offer a major aesthetic improvement over screws and nails.

They offer functional advantages as well: They eliminate splits that can occur when a screw is driven through wood; they don't stain wood the way some screws and nails can; and they don't leave surface depressions where water can pool and damage wood. They avoid the possibility of popped nails—a hazard as well as an eyesore.

Most hidden fasteners are relatively easy to use, though many require under-deck access to attach them. This can present problems in very low-level decks where there isn't sufficient space to work underneath the deck. Other models offer top-surface installation.

Typically, hidden fasteners don't add much to the cost of a deck compared with stainless-steel screws. Hidden fasteners range from 50 cents to $1.25 per square foot of decking.

railings

Railings and stairs often take center stage in a deck design. These important components are closely linked by function and often are the most prominent elements of a deck's appearance. Successful deck projects usually include imaginative designs for railings and stairs so the deck has personality and charm.

Before you begin to design railings, become familiar with your local building codes so that construction complies with all requirements. Remember that it's difficult to design railings and stairs accurately so that all posts and balusters are evenly spaced and all steps are of equal height. If you aren't sure of your

Horizontal Railing Safety: Horizontal railing styles are attractive and particularly appropriate for contemporary homes. Though many codes allow horizontal railings, young children can use the rails as a ladder. If you have young children, and particularly if your deck is more than a few inches off the ground, consider an alternative railing style. Or fasten plexiglass panels between posts. When children are older the panels can be removed.

ABOVE: Purchased from a sail-boat rigging supplier, sturdy but airy stainless-steel cables are used here as horizontal deck rails. The ¼-inch corrosion-resistant cables allow nearly unobstructed views from the deck.

LEFT: Copper pipe, typically used for plumbing, weathers to a dull glow as a railing.

RIGHT: Galvanized aluminum mesh produces a gridded pattern that harmonizes the overall design of this angled deck. The railing provides a practical, long-lasting solution to harsh, salty air.

design abilities, it's best to work with a professional.

SAFETY AND DESIGN

To enhance safety most building codes require railings on decks that are more than 24 inches above the ground. Railings also are key design elements. The most attractive railings harmonize with the style of the house, echoing prominent details or enhancing certain style motifs. The railing on a deck attached to a classic older home, for example, might repeat fanciful trim from an eave or cornice. A railing on a deck attached to a contemporary home might be sleek and simple. A handsome, imaginative railing might not be much more expensive to build than a basic one, and it transforms your deck from an ordinary platform into a striking outdoor living area.

Railings include support posts. To keep railings strong building codes limit the space between railing posts, usually to 4 to 6 feet. The posts along the perimeter of the deck can be a part of the deck's structural system. One end can rest on a footing, and the post can extend up past the decking to be part of

OPPOSITE: The railing design of this cedar deck features beveled spindles on top and lattice below. At the time the deck was built, building codes allowed spindles to be widely spaced.

ABOVE: This ornate railing, with its stately columns, wide stairs, massive railings, and ball-top finials, echoes Victorian style. The baluster design was modified to the required 36-inch height by adding decorative doughnut-like beads at each end.

the railing system. Joists and girders attach to the post below the decking. This type of railing system is especially stable. Otherwise posts are secured separately, usually by bolting the post to the outside of the rim joists.

Between the posts are horizontal elements: the rails. A railing system is

ABOVE: Stainless-steel cabling preserves the view from a deck far better than conventional railing. Its gleaming hardware won't disappear from view completely, however, and adds contemporary flair.

LEFT: A sunburst design gives a long railing character. The specially treated pine used for the railing has the appearance of redwood.

either made entirely of horizontal members called *rails* or can include vertical members called *balusters*. Balusters come in a variety of shapes. The simplest are square; the most decorative are "turned" balusters that have delicate flutes, ridges, and grooves. These basic components can be arranged in many ways to form railings that can be anything from classic to experimental, as long as the final design meets building codes. Most codes require that the space between balusters or rails be no greater than 4 inches.

Railings usually are made of wood, although strong materials, such as steel, copper tubing, and heavy-gauge wire can be used if your construction methods conform to local building codes. Wood can be left natural, stained, or painted. Even with regular applications of clear weather sealers, natural wood will eventually turn a soft, silvery gray. Stained wood shows its grain and is

relatively easy to maintain because preparing the surface with scraping and sanding isn't necessary. Painted wood railings are dramatic and are easy to match or contrast with the color of your house. To minimize repainting use only top-quality exterior paints; applying fresh coats between balusters requires a steady hand and lots of patience.

TOP: **Railings hand-carved from 100-year-old Douglas fir add old-world charm to the first level of a two-story deck when matched with sturdy, rustic 12×12 posts.**

ABOVE: **To take advantage of a great view, have safety glass installed. Coatings such as Diamon-Fusion create a more scratch- and impact-resistant surface and decrease water spotting.**

caps

Cap railings protect the cut ends of railing posts and balusters from the elements while dressing up the appearance of your railing. Caps are typically wider than the rest of the railing and are fastened to the top rail. A wide cap rail adds solidity to a design and makes the space more flexible. If there's not room for additional furnishings and you plan to entertain, wide cap rails can double as resting surfaces for plates and glasses.

In some railing styles the post tops extend above the railing, providing opportunity for further customization with post caps. Post caps are available in various shapes, colors, and materials to suit a plethora of deck and house styles.

Post tops typically come in two basic styles: finials that screw into the top of the post, and caps that have a square base that fits over the top of the post. Most deck finials and caps are designed for 4×4 posts, but be sure to verify the size before selecting a cap. You can find finials and caps in wood and metal. Finial designs range from basic spheres to detailed shapes, such as pineapples. Caps often have decorative metal tops available in various colors.

OPPOSITE TOP: The stylish detailing for this post cap was created with 1×1 pieces of wood that mimic detailing elsewhere in the landscape.

OPPOSITE BOTTOM: In this Arts-and-Crafts-style railing, low-voltage outdoor lights are housed behind translucent panels on the post tops.

RIGHT: On this octagonal deck the table seats only four people, but the large bench and cap rail provide room for more.

BELOW LEFT: The rounded balusters and detailed crowns for these delightful posts, which are topped with copper caps, were fashioned by a router.

BELOW RIGHT: A curved rail wrapping a cantilevered bench makes a welcome addition to a rectangular backyard. The rail serves as a perch for plates when guests sit on benches to dine.

stairs and ramps

A well-designed stairway is expressive, inviting, and safe. Stairs provide a natural, easy transition between your home's interior and your yard. The design should channel traffic away from living spaces and obstructions. Plan a corridor 3 feet wide that leads from exterior doors to the stairs. Make sure that people using the corridor aren't forced to walk around seating areas, cooking stations, and structural members, such as posts.

Stairs can take many forms, but all designs must conform to local building codes. Usually they specify the maximum rise of a step to be 7 ½ inches and the minimum width of a tread to be 10 to 11 inches, for a total rise and run of 17 to 18 inches. Although stairs can't be steeper than specified, usually they can be lower, as long as the design

LEFT: The recessed, railing-free design of these stairs offers a smooth passage from upper to lower level. Well-placed lighting aids movement back and forth at night.

BELOW: A metal railing creates a modern look with lines that complement the angular construction of the deck. The stairs flow from the deck into the landscape, recalling a waterfall in the backyard.

conforms to the codes. A 4-inch-high step, for example, needs a tread 13 to 14 inches wide. Platform steps are a series of shallow decks and work well on gentle slopes where they can hover above the contours of the land.

Stairs for elevated decks require careful consideration. The total run of the stairway can be quite long and might project awkwardly into your yard. To compensate, design stairs that make one or two turns and follow the outside edges of the deck. Stairs built this way can hide posts and other structural members. Stairways that change direction require landings—short platforms at least 3 feet by 3 feet. Larger landings can have built-in seating and planters, creating "interim" decks that complement the overall design.

Stairs for decks usually have "open" risers, with no wood enclosing the vertical, rear part of each step. A system with open risers helps prevent water, leaves, and other debris from accumulating at the intersection of the tread and the riser. This kind of debris can lead to moisture damage and rot.

OPPOSITE: Wide, intricate steps built from 2×2 boards with spacers create visual interest, double as seating, and provide a smooth transition to the flat yard.

Constructing a deck so it is accessible to persons with limited mobility often means building a ramp that accommodates a wheelchair. Your local building department should provide specifications for ramps. A ramp should not have more than 1 inch of rise for every 1 foot of horizontal run. Typically, a ramp should have handrails on either side and be at least 42 inches wide between handrails to allow room for wheelchairs or other mobility aids. Long ramps should include one landing for every 3 feet of vertical rise so that users can pause or have a place to turn around. It's a good idea to provide a concrete slab at the bottom of the ramp for traction.

LEFT: Gently sloping ramps provide wheelchair accessibility to a concrete garden path. The deck's boards lie perpendicular to the slope on the ramps and run diagonally on level sections to improve traction and add visual interest.

BELOW: A wheelchair-accessible ramp is camouflaged by level porch railings that echo the architectural style of a Victorian-era home.

lights

Lighting is the single element that makes an outdoor area as livable by night as it is by day. When creating an outdoor room, lighting should be an integral part of your design. In addition, the right kind of illumination is key in setting the mood of your space. Do you want lighting that provides instant elegance, brightens up casual celebrations, or ensures safety?

Choices for outdoor lighting include chandeliers and sconces, electric floor and table lamps, lanterns, torches, candles, battery-charged canister lights, and strands of white lights. Consider access when selecting the lighting. Electric chandeliers, sconces, and floor and table lamps require outlets. Chandeliers also require an overhead structure, such as a pergola, for mounting.

Small strands of lights beautifully define the perimeter of a rooftop, deck railing, umbrella, or gazebo. Battery-charged or solar-powered canister lights work well when lighting a table or lining the ground. Candles, lanterns, and torches provide romantic light that works anywhere—as long as breezes don't snuff them out.

LEFT: Thanks to the pairing of corner posts with custom lights, a low, sleek bench offers a welcoming perch at dusk. The opalescent glass creates a soft glow.

OPPOSITE: Battery-charged canister lights placed directly on the deck illuminate an outdoor hot tub. The lights don't require unsightly wiring or proximity to an electrical outlet. They do, however, require frequent recharging.

BELOW: Fixtures on your home's exterior allow for uniform lighting. After dark, lights transform an ordinary deck into a magical place.

skirting

Installed under the deck platform along the perimeter of the deck, skirting hides the structural system. It also keeps animals from wandering under your deck and perhaps even nesting there. Skirting usually is made of lath or panels of wood with decorative holes that permit air to circulate, discouraging moisture problems, such as rot or mold. Elaborate skirting can be made of boards, solid panels, or masonry walls with vent holes. Skirting is not a required component; you might decide that your deck looks better without it.

Although skirting is primarily functional, it's a prominent surface and should be considered carefully. Lath panels, for example, compete for attention with stairs and railings. To camouflage skirting stain or paint it a neutral background color, such as gray or dark brown. Bring in foundation plantings that will fill in around your deck and cover at least part of the skirting.

Sketch ideas before committing to a final design. Because the lower edge of the skirting is close to the ground, it should be made from pressure-treated or rot-resistant wood, such as redwood or cedar. Untreated wood needs several coats of a water sealer or preservative before installation.

If possible, install your skirting in individual sections that can be easily removed for maintenance, repair, or replacement. Include a hinged or easily removable section that permits access to the area underneath the deck for inspections and repairs.

BELOW: **Solid walls visually balance a massive deck above. This solid skirting does not reach all the way around the deck, so it does not require ventilation holes to permit air circulation and prevent moisture problems as do other decks with similar skirting.**

ABOVE: Lattice skirting paired with a low limestone border and lush plantings help hide the structural members of this deck. The white skirting matches the trim on the home and the railings on the deck.

LEFT: The white lattice skirting of this free-standing deck serves as a backdrop for the pond and flowerbed that nestle at its base.

built-ins

Built-ins, usually constructed of the same materials as your deck, are cost-effective ways to provide seating, privacy, and staging areas for your favorite activities. Planning built-in benches and planters encourages you to get the most from your outdoor spaces by determining how you'll use your deck and how components will be arranged.

BENCHES

Benches provide permanent seating. A bench's legs and backrest are fastened with bolts directly to the deck's structural components, such as joists or posts. Decking material is cut to fit around it.

Bench seats should be 15 to 18 inches above the floor of the deck, and 15 inches deep. Benches built around the perimeter of a low deck can double as railings. However, if a deck is more than 24 inches above the ground, benches must conform to the building codes that apply to railings. This means that the back of the bench would need to be 36 to 42 inches high to prevent accidents if someone were to stand on the bench seat. Added to the height of the seat, the total height of a back could be 60 inches from the floor of the deck. Be sure to check your local building codes to determine requirements for built-in benches. Built-in benches that are not used as railings can be built in any style.

Be sure to include a reinforcing plate to secure the attachment of the bench to the deck's structural components.

PLANTERS

Planters bring the natural beauty of greenery and flowering plants to deck design. They are permanent structures that should integrate with the overall style of the deck. On low decks they help define the edges or perimeter of the deck and give substance to otherwise

ABOVE: **A large built-in planter and arbor swing serve as focal points on this deck, where portable furnishings coordinate with the built-in furniture.**

BELOW: **Basic deck bench construction provides a sturdy connection between the bench legs and backrest and the structural components of the deck.**

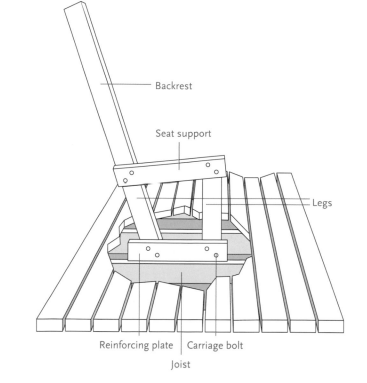

Backrest

Seat support

Legs

Reinforcing plate | Carriage bolt

Joist

plain deck structures. Planters should not be used as a substitute for code-compliant railings.

Make planters from moisture-resistant woods such as cedar, redwood, cypress, or pressure-treated lumber. For annual or perennial flowers, make planters 8 to 12 inches deep. For shrubs, planters should be 18 to 24 inches deep. The planter bottom should have drainage holes that extend completely through the decking material. Bore 1-inch holes every 12 inches throughout the floor of the planter.

To ensure that your planter has a long life and to prevent soils from leaching out and staining decking, line your planter with a waterproof membrane. Use plastic sheeting at least 3 milli-meters thick or 15-pound roofing felt, sometimes called tar paper. Start at the bottom and wrap the membrane up the sides. Overlap edges at least 4 inches. Cut openings in the membrane over the drainage holes. An alternative to plastic sheeting is to coat the interior walls of the planter with roofing tar. Apply it carefully, though, because if it gets on the wood it will stain.

Solid materials, such as fiberglass or galvanized steel, make the best liners. Make fiberglass liners out of flexible fiberglass cloth and paintable hardeners available in a kit for boat repair. A sheet metal shop can prepare custom-made galvanized steel liners to fit exactly inside a planter. It's important to select materials carefully; for example, galvanized steel should not be used with cedar. When both materials are wet and in contact with each other, a chemical reaction occurs that produces stains.

ABOVE: **Built-in planters and side tables flank a deck dominated by a curved bench. The bench is constructed from green 1×2 clear cedar planks, and the planters are made from tongue-and-groove cedar.**

privacy screens

Privacy screens block unwanted views and establish a sense of enclosure in your backyard space. The screens usually aren't solid—latticework or boards spaced several inches apart are enough to create privacy while permitting air circulation.

Privacy screens can be freestanding fences or extensions of a railing system. They should be made of the same material as other deck components so they blend harmoniously with the design. A privacy screen doesn't have to be an enormous wall either. Sometimes a well-placed piece of lattice is all that's needed.

If a screen separates you and a close neighbor, remember how the screen looks from the other side. A well-planned screen takes into account appearances from both sides.

A good way to add privacy is to build a trellis that supports a climbing plant, such as a clematis or trumpet vine. By midsummer both sides of the trellis should fill in with leafy vines brimming with greenery and blossoms.

OPPOSITE: Glass blocks salvaged from an old dairy create a privacy screen. Not every trellis opening is filled—there are just enough blocks to keep out hot rays and wind without sacrificing light and fresh air.

ABOVE: A screen doesn't have to be substantial to be effective. This custom railing doubles as a trellis and provides a comfortable feeling of enclosure and privacy.

BELOW: To block neighbors' views and late-afternoon rays, yellow indoor-outdoor curtains are hung from a west-facing rafter.

overheads

An overhead structure can transform your deck into a Greek temple or a romantic cabana. Overheads provide shade, establish a sense of enclosure, and help define the character and personality of your outdoor room. An overhead usually consists of support posts, rafters, and an open "roof" made of lattice or narrow boards. These structures require few materials and are inexpensive to construct.

Pergolas and arbors are common types of overheads. A pergola is attached to a host structure, such as a house. An arbor is freestanding. Both are excellent for supporting climbing greenery, such as clematis and trumpet vines, that wrap around posts and work their way across lattice to provide shade during the summer. The intricacy of the lattice pattern also determines how much shade the roof offers. To cut the sun's rays effectively, lattice must be closely spaced—no more than about 2 inches apart.

An overhead must be securely fastened to the deck and well-braced between the posts and joists so that the structure remains rigid in the strongest winds. This fastener is called *knee-bracing* or *brackets* and is made of short pieces of lumber fastened at an angle.

Building an overhead is a good way to add flair to your deck and to define individual rooms. Cut the ends of joists into decorative shapes and add curved brackets for stylish touches. Combine your overhead with a trellis or screen to create an outdoor room complete with walls and ceiling.

OPPOSITE: **This simple but solid pergola is constructed to hold the considerable weight of large vines. Petite blue and white ceramic decorations add character.**

BELOW: **An open grid design provides some shade to this deck while still allowing light to filter into the interior of the home. Though the overall effect gives an open feeling, the structure was designed to support the weight of a swing and was wired for electricity.**

ABOVE: **This overhead structure is comprised of large-scale posts and beams. Part of the pergola is more open than the rest, so family members have a choice of sun or shade.**

RIGHT: **Overheads offer opportunities to add flair. Cut rafter ends in decorative shapes to add to your deck's personality. Covered with climbing plants, these overheads furnish some shade.**

LEFT: Overheads can shade specific functional areas, such as dining and spa spaces. Provide other open deck areas for warming in the sun.

BELOW: A pergola doesn't have to be elaborate to be effective. This airy structure blends with the casual style of the seaside home.

outdoor kitchens

LEFT: A low stucco wall with tile accents hosts a grill. The countertop provides functional space for grill prep and storing tools. Another wall surrounding the area serves as shelf space for stacking plates.

OPPOSITE: With two spaces—one for entertaining and dining, the other for cooking and relaxing—this small deck offers everything a family needs for an evening outside. The stone counter built around the grill provides just enough space for the preparation of family meals.

BELOW: All the necessities of an outdoor kitchen, including a refrigerator, sink, and natural gas grill, combine with comfortable seating and a cozy fireplace to create an ideal spot for entertaining.

Cooking centers are increasingly popular. They're typically equipped with short runs of lower cabinets that can withstand outdoor climates. They can hold sinks, gas or electric cooking appliances, and storage compartments for cooking utensils and cleaning supplies. Today's outdoor kitchens often transcend the basics and may even include extra amenities such as built-in bars and fireplaces as well.

Because more people enjoy outdoor cooking and entertaining than ever before, the demand for appliances and kitchen utensils has increased. Many manufacturers have responded with cooktops, refrigerators, rotisseries, and other small appliances that are rated for

safe outdoor use. These appliances feature stainless-steel, anodized aluminum, or enameled bodies that can withstand the rigors of weather and sun.

A cooking center is 34 to 36 inches high and at least 24 inches wide—the same width as a typical lower kitchen cabinet. Cabinets wider than 36 inches are difficult to reach across. Leave 18 inches of countertop workspace on either side of a cooktop or sink. Cabinet bodies and countertops should be able to withstand the weather—solid redwood or cedar are good choices. Otherwise cabinets should be made of exterior- or marine-grade plywood.

Use only weatherproof materials for countertops. Solid-surface countertops

are durable, but might expand and contract with changes in temperature. A professional fabricator should have experience installing solid-surface materials in exterior locations. Tile or stone is a good material if it is rated for exterior use. It should be set on a moisture-resistant base, such as cement tile backer installed over ¾-inch exterior- or marine-grade plywood. Plastic laminate countertops should not be used.

Sinks require care to ensure that pipes do not freeze. Pipes should be insulated, and valves and faucets rated for outdoor use. The best protection against freezing is common sense. When the summer outdoor season is over, drain plumbing lines. If you entertain on a warm fall or spring day, use your indoor kitchen to supply water.

Sensible deck design suggests that cooking centers are made of materials identical or similar to the materials used to construct the deck or painted to match the overall scheme.

Better With Age

Natural wood decks are particularly vulnerable to the elements—rain, sun, mold, and temperature changes take their toll unless decks receive careful attention. Thoughtful design and solid construction, coupled with vigilant maintenance, ensure that even after 15 years this cedar deck still looks as good as new.

The 600-square-foot deck nestles on a steep slope among Douglas fir trees. Constructed of a clear, no-knot cedar known for its ability to resist rot, the deck is kept in shape with annual applications of a non-petroleum-base penetrating wood finish that stains, seals, and protects the deck. In addition, regular sweeping and rinsing keep the deck debris-free.

Multiple outdoor living areas make the most of the sloped backyard. On the deck's upper level, a pergola creates a semi-sheltered spot for outdoor eating near the kitchen's French doors. Accommodating the yard's sideways slope, the lower level is a step down. The jog in design and change in deck-board direction signal the movement from the expanse of open space for outdoor gathering to the area reserved for relaxation and soaking in the sun.

The railing design features beveled spindles on top and lattice below, which offers privacy. When the deck was built, local building codes allowed the spindles to be widely spaced. Before building a similar railing, be sure to check your local codes.

A retaining wall helps shore up the backyard, leaving a plateau filled with small trees, shade plants, and a winding pea gravel path near the deck. On the deck planter boxes and baskets hanging from the pergola's extra-sturdy beams teem with lush shrubs, plants, and flowers, further enhancing the beautiful setting that surrounds the deck.

ABOVE: Small trees and shade plants create a border between the deck and the path that winds past the house.

LEFT: The deck faces northeast, welcoming sun in the morning and shade in the afternoon. The pergola on the upper level provides shade anytime, making it the perfect spot for outdoor dining.

OPPOSITE: Regular maintenance makes this deck look new. The large size of the deck, with its different levels and timeless design, accommodates the homeowners' changing needs.

Stepping Up, Expanding Out

When a simple rectangular deck evolves into a series of outdoor areas, there's little reason to spend time inside. A gazebo at one end and a swim spa at the other anchor this remodeled redwood deck, while a series of staircases facilitates the transition from level to level.

On one side of the sprawling 2,000-square-foot deck, the elevated, octagonal gazebo echoes the angles of the bay windows overlooking the deck. The gazebo showcases views of the Rocky Mountains in the distance and provides a shady retreat for dining and relaxing.

To further the three-dimensional outdoor space, an 8×16 swim spa integrates into the deck opposite the gazebo. Instead of framing the exposed spa, which would have exaggerated its size, the homeowners placed it on a concrete slab foundation and built the redwood deck around it, creating the look of a recessed pool.

Near the spa a convenient outdoor cooking center contains a gas grill with a side burner, as well as a small refrigerator for condiments, snacks, and drinks. Ample decking makes this area another gathering place for relaxing or watching the kids splash around.

To transition between the original deck and the flanking outdoor areas, short, wide staircases lead from the gazebo area to spa deck to ground level. Cedar balusters with 1×1 pickets and routed caps surround the deck for safety while creating an airy look that doesn't impede views of the landscape.

The spa deck isn't built flush to the house. Instead, the structure is set out several feet, allowing light to filter into the walk-out basement's windows below. This covered lower-level area features a hammock for lounging. Built-ins provide more seating and storage space.

Although the series of outdoor areas within this multilevel playstation require ample space, the same principles could be applied to expanding any deck—avoid the one-dimensional by planning multiple areas to accommodate all your needs.

OPPOSITE: **Toward hot tub and gazebo: Wide steps transition between the deck's multilevel rooms. The uppermost level includes a gazebo and table for shaded dining. The original portion of the deck in the center is perfect for relaxing in the sun. The lowest level includes a cooking area and swim spa.**

TOP: **Anchored by a gazebo at one end and a swim spa at the other, the multilevel redwood deck gracefully passes from house to yard.**

LEFT: **Hidden below the original deck, another outdoor room is accessed through the walk-out basement. A hammock hangs near a rock-lined waterfall; benches provide seating as well as storage.**

ing. The 4,500-gallon koi pond is surrounded by 32 tons of granite boulders, many of which are used to create a waterfall. Plants that blend with the surroundings, including an evergreen bonsai, contribute calm. Details such as a Japanese-inspired granite lantern and a mini Japanese teahouse used as a birdhouse complete the aura that pervades the peaceful outdoor space.

OPPOSITE: **Plantings with an unadorned Zen-like look—including bonsai, bamboo, and ornamental grass—bring calm to the setting.**

LEFT: **The deck's design is a piece of living art visible from the main areas of the home. The furniture and decking blend with the prominent cedar siding of the house.**

BELOW: **Set among the trees, the simple yet elegant deck blends function with nature.**

Most Japanese gardens follow the principles of clean lines and open, uncluttered space. Inspired by nature and infused with Zen-like atmosphere, this three-level deck satisfies the demand for a tranquil gathering area removed from distractions of contemporary life.

Intuition and the topography of the site guided the shaping of the project—no design blueprints were needed. Already blending with its surroundings, the house is situated where tall conifers anchor the landscape. Stone stairs lead from the house to the deck. A koi pond and the deck's three levels nestle among tall stands of evergreens and effortlessly hug the shape of the land, delivering 600 square feet of open-air living without forcing the removal of trees.

The pleasing multilevel deck was constructed as a series of cedar rectangles built low to the ground. A railing-free design and natural materials allow man-made components to seamlessly transition into nature. To enhance the experience, outdoor stereo speakers tucked out of sight and timer-controlled lights enable the deck to be used for relaxing or entertaining, night and day.

Even the plantings surrounding the deck are low and unobtrusive. The trees provide height but aren't too dense to block all sunlight. For privacy, a living fence of bamboo sprouts along the property line.

The mix of elements built on a Japanese garden theme creates a lovely place for contemplation and entertain-

basics of deck building

Understanding the fundamentals of deck building helps you communicate with professionals to get the results you want. »

>> A deck project has several phases. Knowing what to expect during each phase will help you prepare for the next, enabling the project to proceed as smoothly as possible. The process includes essentials, such as soliciting bids, hiring a contractor, and signing contracts. Understanding what each phase involves will help ensure you make the best choices.

building phases

Building a deck could take as little as a week or as long as several months, depending on the size and complexity of the design, as well as unpredictable events, such as weather delays. Despite these variables, most deck construction follows a basic sequence: preparing the site; installing the foundation; building the structural system; adding decking, railings, and stairs; and finishing the job with protective sealers, stains, or paints. While methods can vary from builder to builder, the essential process is straightforward. Becoming familiar with these steps helps you make necessary decisions and anticipate problems so that the job proceeds smoothly and efficiently.

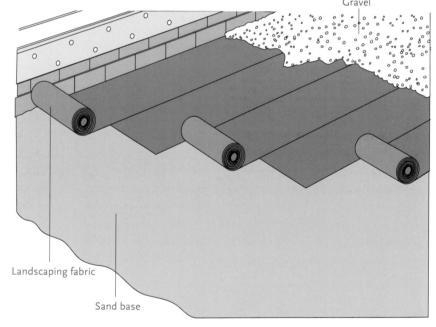

Gravel

Landscaping fabric

Sand base

ABOVE: Suppress the growth of unwanted vegetation by installing landscaping fabric over the building site. Install the fabric over a sand bed 1 to 2 inches thick, then cover the fabric with gravel to conceal it.

OBTAINING PERMITS

Any structure attached to a main house—and often any freestanding structure—requires a building permit before construction can begin. Permits are issued after a member of the local building or planning department reviews your plans and evaluates them for safety and structural integrity. If an architect didn't produce your plans, you can have them reviewed by a registered structural engineer before submitting them to a building department. This is especially helpful if your deck is complex. Plan to spend $300 to $600 for a structural engineer to review your

plans and make suggestions that will address challenges.

Your plans also must meet local setback requirements. Setbacks determine allowable distance from property lines for new construction. You may be able to apply for a variance that allows you to build within a setback zone. Your application must argue compelling reasons for the variance, such as the construction of a wheelchair ramp.

Your building department can tell if your property includes any rights-of-way, which are corridors that allow utility companies or neighbors legal

access through parts of your property. You cannot build in right-of-way areas.

INSPECTIONS

Expect two or three visits from a local building inspector during construction. The inspector examines the structure to ensure that it's being built safely and is in compliance with local codes.

Ask the inspector at what stages he or she expects to visit your site, and plan to be on-site so you can answer questions.

Don't be intimidated: Most building inspectors are knowledgeable and helpful. Their main concern is safety, and most are quite willing to talk about your specific plans and construction methods to ensure that your deck project is built soundly and on schedule.

UTILITIES
Notify utility, cable television, and phone companies about your plans for building a deck. Ask them to mark the underground locations of wires, cables, pipes, and sewer lines. Most companies provide this service for free or a small fee.

SITE PREPARATION
Once the plans are finalized and approved by the building department, work can begin. Any obstructions, such as shrubs, outbuildings, or small trees that are not included in the design, must be removed from the construction site. Soil near the foundation should be graded so it slopes away from the house at a rate of about 6 vertical inches for every 3 horizontal feet. To suppress the

growth of unwanted vegetation underneath the deck, cover the area with landscaping fabric. First add a layer of coarse sand for drainage. Then cover the sand with landscaping fabric. Bury the fabric under several inches of gravel. It's more efficient to do this after all footings have been poured.

FOUNDATION WORK
If the deck is attached to the house, the location of the ledger is marked on the side of the house. Using the ledger location as a reference, the deck is outlined with a system of strings pulled tautly over staked batterboards. These string lines establish the edges of the deck and create reference corners. Once the deck is outlined with lines, the strings locate and mark the placement of foundation footings.

After all footing locations are marked, the holes must be dug. For small decks the holes can be dug with a hand-operated clamshell digger. For larger decks with more than six or seven footing holes, consider renting a power auger. This awkward, heavy tool is not easy to master, but it makes short work of digging holes. A power auger can dig a 10-inch-wide hole 42 inches deep in

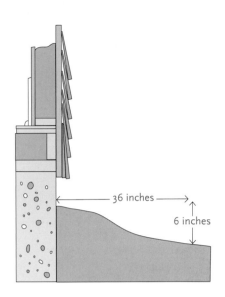

two or three minutes, depending on how hard the soil is.

MAIN CONSTRUCTION
After the preliminary work is completed and the foundation is poured and allowed to cure, the construction of a deck should proceed systematically. Posts, girders, and joists are installed, and braced if necessary. The substructure usually is fastened together with galvanized metal connectors that hold the members securely and provide strength at the joints. Decking is laid over the joists and fastened with galvanized nails or screws. Stairs, railings, and ancillary structures, such as overheads, are added. A protective sealer, stain, or paint completes the work.

ABOVE: It's important that the soil next to the foundation is graded so that water drains away from foundation walls. The soil should slope at least 6 vertical inches over a distance of 3 horizontal feet.

LEFT: Deck construction usually begins with the installation of the ledger. From the ledger, layout strings stretched taut over batter boards ensure that the deck structure will be straight and square. Post locations are marked using a plumb bob.

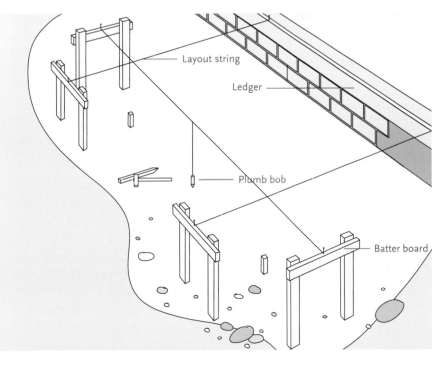

building plans

A good set of building plans allows you to realize the deck of your dreams and ensures that the work is completed to code. Building plans document details of the construction process, from the location of foundation footings to the placement of pipes for water and electricity. Initially you collected clippings, photographs, and brochures to assist you with designing a space that meets your needs. Your design professional works with you to develop the map for these dreams: the building plans. Before getting bids and hiring a contractor, you may need to have a registered structural engineer review and approve the plans.

MEETING CODES

Once the building plans for the deck are complete, have a number of copies made. Take a set of the plans and a materials list to the building department. The building inspector may ask for changes or clarifications but is less likely to do so if your plans are blueprints from a registered architect or have been approved by a registered structural engineer.

DIRECTING THE WORK

Approved building plans are critical to the accurate completion of work. The general contractor and subcontractors refer to the plans as they excavate, build, and put finishing touches on the new deck. Make several copies of the blueprints so you have enough for everyone involved in the project, and keep a copy for yourself. Refer to your plans regularly as you inspect the project to make sure construction is progressing as

you planned. Some plans have a legend to explain abbreviations and symbols. If you don't know what a symbol or an abbreviation means, ask.

ABOVE: **Detailed and accurate building plans are critical, particularly when faced with a complicated site and deck design such as this steep slope and lap pool surround.**

hiring a contractor

Unless you have plenty of time to devote to a project and are an accomplished do-it-yourselfer, hire a professional building contractor. (See page 157 for more information about do-it-yourself considerations.) Take the time to choose a contractor who has a good reputation and whom you feel comfortable with.

A licensed contractor has completed state requirements to perform various types of work. General contractors usually have a broad knowledge of all aspects of construction and are hired to organize and complete a job according to an agreed-upon schedule. Specialized contractors, such as electrical contractors, are called subcontractors. Electrical contractors, for example, have passed state certification programs that permit them to perform work relating to electrical hookups. It is your general contractor's responsibility to hire all necessary subcontractors.

To find a qualified general contractor in your area:

• Ask friends, neighbors, or colleagues for the names of reliable contractors they have hired. Get several names.

• Meet with prospective contractors to discuss your project. Ask about their experience with building decks and what problems they have encountered. Ask for a ballpark figure for your project. This figure isn't a precise bid and should not be regarded as an agreement. But discussing money at an early stage may give you an idea of how knowledgeable a contractor is and how comfortable he or she is discussing costs.

• Ask how long the contractor has been in business and if he or she carries insurance. Without insurance you are liable for accidents that occur on your property. Contractors should have a certificate of insurance to cover damage, liability, and workers' compensation. It is

acceptable to request that you see the certificate before proceeding.

• Obtain references from contractors and take the time to inspect recent work they've done as well as work from five to eight years ago so you can ask questions about how their work has held up. Reliable contractors should provide this

information readily and will be proud to have their work on display. Check with your local Better Business Bureau to see if any unresolved complaints are on file.

• Narrow your choices to five contractors and ask for final bids. (See "Getting Bids," page 108.) Make sure all contractors have similar deadlines for submitting bids—about three weeks should be sufficient. Eliminate any contractor who posts a late bid.

• Carefully review each bid to see how thoroughly they have been researched. A bid should include the specified fee—usually 10 to 15 percent of the total costs. Be skeptical of any bid that seems significantly lower than others—the lowest bidder will not necessarily give the most satisfying results.

• When it comes to a final selection, take all factors into account. Remember that price isn't the only consideration; personality, quality, workmanship, and professionalism are all factors to consider.

Once you find your contractor, keep communication open. Schedule regular meetings to discuss progress and stay informed about interim deadlines. Tell your contractor that you don't expect to make your final payment until the job has passed all required building inspections, you have seen written proof that all subcontractors and suppliers have been paid, and you and your contractor have walked through the project and agree that the job is complete.

Working With a Contractor:
Once you've hired a contractor and signed the contract, you'll be in close quarters with this person for the duration of the project. To achieve the best results, follow these tips:

Communication is key. If you are displeased with anything, tell the contractor immediately. The longer you wait, the more difficult and expensive the corrections. Similarly, when you are especially pleased with results, let your contractor know. Even though you are hiring the person to do good work, compliments can go a long way toward getting top-quality results.

Document changes in writing. Though you want to minimize changes—they are generally costly—you may need to alter plans after work has started. Any change-work agreements should be as precise and detailed as the original contract.

Coordinate schedules. Try to be at home briefly when the contractors arrive. That way you can quickly assess the work done the previous day and discuss any decisions. Once the contractors have started work for the day, plan to be out of the construction area to avoid delaying work.

getting bids

Once you have narrowed your list of prospective contractors, you need to get final bids from each. If you hire a general contractor, that person needs to get bids from subcontractors. In either case, you have responsibilities to secure a carefully prepared bid for the project.

Begin by gathering all planning documents. Most critical is a detailed drawing, preferably a blueprint, and a materials list. Blueprints are copies of original drawings by a registered architect or structural engineer, but a qualified designer or even the homeowner can create usable plans. Blueprints from a registered architect or structural engineer can be given directly to a contractor for bids, but plans produced by a designer or home-owner must first be reviewed, approved, and stamped by a registered designer or structural engineer.

The materials list should be as com-plete and comprehensive as possible. It should specify the quantity and brand names of materials needed and the brand names and model numbers of fixtures and appliances to be installed. If specific companies are not identified, the contractor will furnish brands of his or her preference.

Many homeowners enjoy being involved in the selection process and like to shop for certain items themselves. Be sure your contractor understands your intentions and that the materials list indicates any purchases you intend to make. This information should be included in the contract. (See "Making a Contract," page 109.) Both you and your contractor must agree about any possi-ble limitations because of size, weight, and other factors.

When bids start to arrive, study them to determine how each was pre-pared and carefully examine the level of detail each contractor provides. A metic-ulously prepared bid usually indicates that the contractor has carefully consid-ered your project and is prepared for potential problems.

A bid should include itemized mate-rials lists, itemized figures for installation work, and a timeline with stages of com-pletion clearly defined. The best contractors offer a discount for work that is not completed in a reasonable period. There also should be an agreed-upon rate for change orders. Change orders occur when the homeowner decides to alter the plan or type of materials specified. Although most contractors will work with clients to make minor changes, some alterations cause work delays that disrupt shipping arrangements or cause contractors to alter schedules with other jobs. The best way to avoid changes is to plan thoroughly, well in advance.

If all the bids vary widely, review each with the contractor who prepared it to discover why. It may be that certain items or tasks have been omitted from some of the bids. Make sure all the prospective contractors are working with identical information and plans.

ABOVE: **Before embarking on a project that should net results such as this deck retreat, secure bids from several contrac-tors. Review the bids carefully to ensure that they encompass all the work you want completed. If amenities, such as the built-in bench and planter, are included in one bid, make sure they are factored into other bids.**

making a contract

Once you have selected a contractor, you should sign a written contract. Many contractors have prepared forms. If you are unsure about the specific points of a contract, consult a lawyer.

Contracts are not all alike; but a good contract should cover these points:

• A precise description of all work to be completed by the contractor and subcontractors and a description of all materials to be installed. The description of materials and finishes should include the specific types and brands.

• The total cost of the job, including all materials, labor, and fees.

• A schedule of payments that you make to the contractor. Beware of contracts asking for large up-front payments—some states even limit the amount of up-front payments made to contractors before work begins.

• A work schedule with dates specified for the completion of each stage of the project. The schedule should include an allowance for delays caused by delivery problems, weather, and product back orders. The schedule of payments should coordinate with the dates specified for the completion of each stage.

• A right of rescission that allows homeowners to back out of the contract within 72 hours of signing.

• A certificate of insurance that guarantees the contractor has appropriate coverage.

• A warranty that guarantees that materials and construction are free from defects for a certain period, usually one year.

• An arbitration clause that specifies the precise method you will use to settle disputes.

• A description of change-order procedures stating what happens if you decide to alter plans after the contract has been signed. The description should include a fee structure.

• A release of liens to ensure that homeowners won't incur liens or charges

Be Thorough: Make certain the contract details all aspects of the project. If, for example, an old patio needs to be removed prior to construction of the deck and you'd like the builder to handle the demolition and removal, state that in the contract rather than relying on a verbal agreement. If you'll take responsibility for some aspects of the project to save money, include those homeowner responsibilities in the contract too. Even when you're working with reputable companies, it's best to have details in writing to avoid any misunderstandings.

against the property as a result of legal actions filed against the contractor or subcontractors .

LEFT: Anytime you involve outside professionals, a contract is important. In the case of this deck and elaborate fireplace, the contract should specify details about all aspects, including who is responsible for what work.

planning a spa

Decks are great border areas for swimming pools and spas. Decks make comfortable surfaces for bare feet, and the weather-resistant nature of decking materials makes them good surfaces for surrounding a pool or spa. Some synthetic materials (see pages 64-65) include textured surfaces ideal for areas that might get wet. You'll need to plan for electrical and plumbing systems and for equipment, such as water heaters and filters. If located beneath the deck, equipment should be accessible through a removable or hinged panel.

DECKS FOR POOLS

Besides being ideal pool surrounds, decks are easily configured to provide areas for sunning and sitting or to allow access to an aboveground swimming pool. Add privacy screens, overhead shade structures, and cabanas for storing pool toys. Place mechanical equipment, such as pumps and filters, behind a screen to hide them from view.

Cedar and redwood tend to be more splinter-free than pressure-treated wood, although they are more expensive. Because it is constantly exposed to moisture, even weather-resistant poolside decking requires special care. Coat both sides of decking with a water sealant before installation. Plan to reseal the boards annually for top performance.

Remember that most building codes require pools to be surrounded by childproof fences and gates. Check with your local building department to ensure that you incorporate any protective measures into your final plans.

ADDING A SPA OR HOT TUB

Determine the best location for your spa based on privacy and access to your house and whether you want your tub in a shady or sunny location. If your

property offers views, orient your tub to take advantage of them.

A typical round hot tub is 6 feet in diameter and occupies 30 square feet. A rectangular tub takes up about 48 square feet. Plan additional space for sitting and unobstructed space at least 36 inches wide that allows you to walk around the tub easily—a total of 100 to 150 square feet of deck space.

When full of water, a hot tub may weigh 2 tons. A typical deck won't support that much weight, so plan for an independent foundation that is engineered by a qualified professional. If you plan to set a tub onto an existing deck, restructure the supporting lumber and add a foundation underneath the tub. Some building codes require that tubs be protected by a fence with a childproof gate that restricts access to the tub area. If a fence and gate are not possible, substitute an approved tub cover with childproof latches.

ABOVE: **A spa requires an independent foundation to support its weight. The foundation is poured before the deck is constructed. If neighbors have a clear view of the spa, plan for a screen to ensure privacy.**

Any wood—even pressure-treated wood—will dry out, crack, and turn gray if left exposed to the elements. To keep your deck looking its best, finish your deck with a clear water-repellent sealer, a stain, or paint. To ensure long life, treat all surfaces of decking boards before installation.

Pressure-treated wood used for structural components resists weathering. If it turns gray and displays some minor cracks, it usually is hidden from view and won't detract from the beauty of your deck. Even so, it's a good idea to finish the ends of structural lumber with a water sealer. The chemicals used to produce pressure-treated lumber some-times don't soak all the way to the center of the boards. Treating the ends protects against moisture penetration and ensures the longest possible life for your deck.

BELOW: A deck with two kinds of finishes is common and requires two maintenance schedules. In this case, the cedar decking should be cleaned and resealed once a year, while the painted railings need recoating about every three years.

finishing

CLEAR FINISHES

Clear finishes seal wood against moisture and help prolong its beauty. Clear finishes with ultraviolet (UV) blockers help prevent wood from turning gray, but after many years some graying is inevitable. The best way to keep wood decking looking fresh is to scrub it thoroughly at least once a year with a commercial deck-cleaning agent designed to restore the natural color. Then seal the decking. Clear finishes with mildewcide, a water-repellent preservative, help prevent the growth of surface mildew.

STAINS

Alter the appearance of a deck with stains or paints especially formulated for decking. Oil-base and water-base stains color the wood and protect it from moisture and sun. Semitransparent stains let the grain pattern show through. Solid stains hide the grain and mask flaws. Test the stain on a scrap piece to make sure you like the appearance. You can stain pressure-treated wood, but because it already is impregnated with a color—either green

or brown—it's especially important to test scrap pieces before committing to the final look. Stain reapplied every two or three years freshens the appearance of the deck. Clean the deck thoroughly before reapplying stain.

PAINTS

Deck paints are specially formulated to withstand weather. As with any paint, exposure to the elements eventually will result in cracking and peeling. Maintaining the appearance of painted surfaces requires periodic scraping, sanding, and recoating.

If specified by the manufacturer, deck paints resist foot traffic and can be used on decking boards. However, this is a harsh test even for the most durable paint. To add color, consider painting railings, fascia, overheads, and built-ins, and finishing decking boards with clear sealers or stains.

FINISHING TECHNIQUES

Decking materials should be dry before painting—but not too dry. Left in the sun without protection, the moisture

content of lumber will evaporate quickly, often resulting in split, warped wood. But in other cases, decking materials are often freshly milled and full of moisture, making it difficult for sealers or stains to penetrate the grain. Timing is key. Wood is ready for finishing if it quickly absorbs a few drops of water sprinkled on its surface.

Before finishing, cover nearby plants, structures, and landscaping features with plastic sheets or drop cloths. Apply sealers, stains, and paints with a brush, a roller, or a sprayer. A roller attached to an extension pole allows you to stand while working, shortening application time. A sprayer coats quickly but sometimes unevenly. Watch for dry spots and recoat them if necessary. Spread puddles with a brush or roller to evenly distribute the finish.

Avoid painting if the weather is very hot or humid. Either condition can cause the paint to fail to adhere properly. Always use a top-quality primer as the initial coat. Latex primers work well and clean up easily, but oil primers penetrate the wood more completely, creating a tighter, longer-lasting bond.

BELOW LEFT: **Most sealers or stains can be applied with a paint roller—just be sure to let each coat dry before applying another.**

BELOW RIGHT: **Test your deck to see if it is sealed properly by sprinkling water on the surface. If it beads up and does not soak in within two minutes, the board is sealed well enough.**

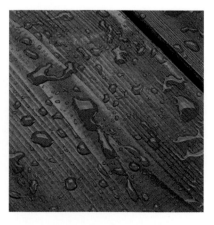

maintenance

It's inevitable—sun, rain, and foot traffic are certain to damage the surface of your deck no matter how well you care for it. Treat your deck just as you would any other investment. With regular maintenance it will be the fabulous focal point of your backyard for years.

Keep an eye on your deck year-round. Regularly brush off fallen leaves and clean between decking board cracks, paying attention to corners where silt and grime can collect. Undertake a major cleaning each spring and fall. Inspect for damage, clean off debris with a hose, sand any splinters, and use a stain remover to lift grill or dirt stains. Scrub the deck to remove dirt, mildew, and moss.

Clean the entire deck—not just the parts that appear dirty. If you use a homemade cleaning solution, keep in mind that cleaner with bleach lightens the wood's natural hue; a nonbleach cleaner removes dirt and stains without affecting color. Wet the deck with a hose, then use a stiff scrub brush or

broom to work the solution into the wood before rinsing. To reduce the elbow grease required, try a manufactured deck wash that chemically cleans the wood.

If your deck still doesn't come clean, try a pressure washer. Be sure to use a fan tip with the washer. Avoid rotating tips, which spin at the nozzle, because they can tear up the wood. Take care not to strip away the soft grain of the wood when cleaning; you may wish to hire a professional to clean the deck so this doesn't occur.

Make certain you're buying the right stain for your deck. Clear stain allows the wood's natural beauty to shine through but requires restaining every 12 to 18 months. If you would rather stain once every three to four years, select a semitransparent or tinted stain. Stains with pigments in the oil better resist UV damage. Avoid using exterior paint on deck boards; it provides minimal protection.

Let the deck dry for at least 24 hours before you apply sealer or stain. Using a stain when the deck is wet means the oil won't penetrate the wood; the stain will just sit on the surface. Apply the stain on a cool day, when it has time to soak into the decking before the sun gets too harsh. Cover as much of the wood as possible, including the ends.

ABOVE: **Living next to the ocean does have one drawback—constant breezes carry salt air that causes erosion. To combat this, saline-tolerant redwood decking and bronze railing were used.**

5

transitions

Harmonize your deck with its surroundings.
Integrate landscaping and other hardscapes to
create a pleasing outdoor living space. >>

>> The appeal of an inviting, well-designed deck derives from the structure, its amenities, and also from what surrounds it. Placing landscaping around your deck creates a relaxing outdoor environment. As you enjoy your deck, your pleasure will come from the space itself, as well as what you see as you gaze beyond.

deck to yard

A smooth transition between your new deck and the surrounding yard is both aesthetic and functional. Functionally, you will enjoy your entire outdoor area more if the space beyond your deck is a natural extension of the deck. Aesthetically, creating a pleasing transition between the deck and yard is about the view from the deck to the yard beyond and vice versa.

Decks are outdoor living spaces with features and amenities of the indoors that invite relaxation and entertaining. With proper planning the area beyond your deck becomes a natural extension of the indoor space.

The planning begins with the design of the deck itself. Proper design of the deck includes entryways from your home to the deck and from the deck to the yard. Landscaping the surrounding area expands your potential uses of the yard and adds to your enjoyment.

Utilize hardscapes. Plan patios that transition between the deck and yard, as well as defined access points, such as steps, paths, and walkways. Transitions from the deck to yard are particularly key with a raised deck. An adjacent patio allows traffic to easily flow from the deck, across the patio, and into the yard. This type of configuration also provides additional options for large gatherings. Paths or walkways that lead

Multilevel Decks: A multilevel deck provides an ideal solution to the problems presented by sloping yards. On this three-tiered deck, each level functions as an outdoor living space. Thanks to the deck, the once-rocky, unusable land is now an entertainment area. The decking conforms to the natural terrain instead of fighting it. Because of the step-up design, the deck itself functions as a stairway through the yard.

Transitioning from a high second-story deck to the yard is a challenge. Some second-level decks forgo direct lawn access completely, forcing a trip through the house to access one from the other. Here, a sweeping wood-and-iron staircase offers a graceful descent from deck to backyard and ensures more usage of both spaces.

BELOW: Wide stairs leading from the deck to the lawn serve a trio of purposes: They allow for easy traffic flow between the yard and deck, provide additional impromptu seating for large gatherings, and offer a staging ground for attractive potted plants.

from the deck to the surrounding yard and gardens encourage you and your visitors to enjoy the full pleasures of the outdoors.

Consider the sights and sounds. Most likely you will spend much of your time on the deck gazing out into the yard. Perhaps the deck takes advantage of a breathtaking view, such as a distant mountain range. More likely your gaze falls on your neighbor's house. Create your own visual interest by breaking up a large expanse of lawn with a garden, trellis, or outdoor sculpture. Install a bubbling fountain just off the deck. The soothing gurgle of water will provide a pleasant background sound.

Create continuity. The transition between your home, deck, and yard will feel and look more natural if you choose materials, colors, and plants that are related. If you plant a garden within viewing distance, include a few of the same plants you used in the foundation plantings surrounding the deck or in planters on the deck.

pathways

Pathways are natural methods to access key features of the yard from your new deck. Paths and walkways are practical, directing traffic and minimizing damage to the lawn that occurs along unmarked, but often frequented, paths. Careful planning of pathways expands the use of your entire outdoor space.

Consider bordering a walkway leading from your deck with plants that are inviting to the touch. Ferns, soft-needled conifers, and some ornamental grasses are good options. Avoid planting thorny or spiky plants right along the pathway and deck railing. Stray stems may scratch.

ABOVE AND LEFT: **Gravel-covered paths that widen into seating areas expand the living space from the deck throughout the yard. The pathways also divide the yard into smaller, more manageable, and intimate garden rooms. Gravel is a low-maintenance choice for pathways and it drains quickly after rains. If gravel paths will abut a lawn, consider installing raised edging, such as the bricks in this landscape, to keep gravel from spilling over into the grass.**

LEFT: Pathways don't have to be limited to the yard. This walkway conveniently connects the two main areas of this deck. Cable railing provides eye-pleasing variety from the other decking, visually indicates a different use of that portion of the deck, and affords an unobstructed view from the living room window (on the right).

LEFT AND BELOW: Broad pathways consisting of a series of small, multilevel decks connect intimate niches, such as this tranquil pond. The decks tidily connect various outdoor rooms, including this fire pit with built-in benches, much like interior hallways connect the spaces inside a home.

Light the Way: Installing path lights creates a nighttime visual treat from your deck and allows safe passage along pathways. Select path lights as part of an overall lighting scheme for a coordinated look and the most pleasing results.

deck and patio
combinations

Decks and patios are staples of outdoor living. Integrate the two and you have a grand space for outdoor enjoyment. A deck and patio combination can extend your family room into the outdoors to take full advantage of nature, sun, and fresh air. The right combination functions as a transitional space that blends the best of indoor and outdoor life. Particularly when paired with a raised deck, a patio offers a graceful transition from the higher deck down to the yard, plus the added benefit of additional outdoor living space.

PLANNING

Before pouring a pad of concrete next to the deck and calling it a patio, consider how you want to use your entire outdoor space. Work on a complete design for both the deck and patio, as well as surrounding areas. Consider how you want and need the entire space to function. Do you imagine an extravagant entertainment center with dining areas and extensive seating for guests? Do you envision a luxurious spa complete with a hot tub, swimming pool, and shady cabana?

BRICK. Durability: Good. **Color Choices:** Organic reds, tans, browns, grays. **Base Required:** Dry-fit over gravel and sand base, or mortared over concrete. **Ease of Installation:** Dry-fit is relatively easy; mortared requires skill.

FLAGSTONE. Durability: Good. **Color Choices:** Reds, creams, yellows, grays, dark blues, browns, some variations. **Base Required:** Dry-fit over gravel and sand base, or mortared over concrete. **Ease of Installation:** Dry-fit is relatively easy; mortared requires skill.

QUARRY TILE. Durability: Excellent. **Color Choices:** Organic reds, tans, browns, grays. **Base Required:** Mortar and grout over concrete. **Ease of Installation:** Requires skill.

CONCRETE SLAB. Durability: Excellent. **Color Choices:** Dull gray; can be colored. **Base Required:** Gravel and sand base. **Ease of Installation:** Simple but labor-intensive.

CONCRETE PAVER. Durability: Excellent. **Color Choices:** Organic reds, tans, browns, grays. **Base Required:** Dry-fit over gravel and sand base, or mortared over concrete. **Ease of Installation:** Dry-fit is relatively easy; mortared requires skill.

UNGLAZED CERAMIC TILE. Durability: Excellent. **Color Choices:** Unlimited. **Base Required:** Mortar and grout over concrete. **Ease of Installation:** Requires skill.

Make the most of a deck and patio combination through careful planning. Consider how the structures will work together. Explore the materials available for patios. Which materials blend and complement the style of your deck, home, and landscape?

The size and style of the patio paired with your deck should depend on how you plan to use the area. If you entertain often, the entire space should be large enough for guests to comfortably converse, mingle, and dine. If the area is to be used only for occasional family barbecues or for relaxing and reading, the patio can be fairly small. Make sure to take into account the total space of both the deck and the patio.

LEFT: **Contrasting colors distinguish the entertaining and soaking areas on the deck from the patio that transitions from the deck to the yard. Using dark stain on the deck visually links it to the similar-hued house. Positioning the spa on the deck near the house shortens the journey through chilly breezes and makes it easy to connect the spa to the home's electrical and plumbing systems.**

OPPOSITE: **Stairs lead from a hot-tub room to a colorful patio floor. The redwood deck's gray stain ties the structures to the hardscaping. Further easing the transition, a small waterfall built from concrete and gray basalt and surrounded by long-blooming flowers borders the stairs.**

A deck and patio combination can help define spaces for specific use. If the deck is easily accessible from the kitchen, for example, design the deck for alfresco dining, with chairs and a table large enough for comfortable meals. The adjacent patio, nestled into a backdrop of mature trees, might be ideal as a cozy sitting area outfitted with a chaise longue and side table. In this case both the placement and the furnishings indicate usage.

Consider placement of the deck and patio. Typically a deck would be adjacent to the house, with the patio extending from the deck into the yard. However, if the area next to the house is flat but the yard extends to a sharp slope farther out, you may want to position a patio near the house, where the terrain is conducive to it, and vault a deck over the slope to create more usable outdoor living space.

FINISHING AND MAINTENANCE

Just as with a deck, a patio requires proper finishing and maintenance to keep it looking its best. Many kinds of stone and unglazed tiles are porous. Depending on the type of material, their surfaces absorb water. This means they can be stained by spills, dirt, wet leaves, and rusting metal, such as grills. To prevent staining and to keep patio surfaces looking fresh, stone and tile surfaces should be finished with the right kind of sealer. Your tile or stone manufacturer should be able to recommend sealers.

Bricks, concrete, and concrete pavers are impervious to moisture and temperature fluctuations and usually do not require sealers.

Sweep floors frequently to remove grit. Any spills should be cleaned as soon as possible to minimize the possibility of staining. For information about maintaining decks, see page 113.

ABOVE: An expansive deck with a gazebo partners with a small brick patio that doubles as a walkway to connect the main deck with a smaller one. A rocky stream bed provides storm drainage for the sloping lot. Brick was selected for the patio to coordinate with the home's exterior.

OPPOSITE: A small deck raised to the height of the home's interior opens to a large patio of concrete pavers. The patio is graded with a 2 percent slope away from the house for easy runoff. Because the homeowners are avid gardeners, with an 8,500-square-foot garden around their home, a large, raised deck wasn't appropriate. Instead, the patio easily transitions to a series of ground-level paths that wind through the gardens.

Base Gravel: Gravel used as the base for patio construction typically is called class-5 gravel or $^3/_4$-inch highway gravel. It is a mixture of small, irregularly shaped pieces that fit together tightly when tamped. Don't order pea gravel—it won't settle into a firm base—even if you're planning to cover the under-portion of your deck with it. Enough gravel to make a base 4 inches deep for a small, 10×10-foot patio would weigh approximately 2$^1/_2$ tons.

deck-and-
screen-porch combinations

Screen porches can provide the best of indoor and outdoor living—fresh air and breezes without pesky bugs. Enclose a portion of a deck to create a screen porch and couple it with open deck space, and you've expanded the options for outdoor living. If it's raining or too many bugs are joining your feast, move to the screen porch. When you want to enjoy the sun's warming rays or gather around a fire pit, move to the open deck.

Screening a portion of a deck is relatively inexpensive. Screen porches generally have a substructure similar to a deck, with a ledger attached to the house and joists supporting the decking or floorboards. Depending on what type of structure you want to support the screening, the deck must be capable of withstanding the new loads imposed upon it. Lightweight screen frames and a standard roof should weigh no more than a gazebo or any other overhead

often built on decks, and should pose no structural concerns. If you plan an elaborate screened structure, involve an architect to be certain the deck is designed to support it.

Check local codes for screen porch requirements. In most areas, if the deck and screened area are more than 30 inches above grade (ground), the structure will require railings or guardrails at least 36 inches high. Screens and basic framing alone are not sufficient to meet this requirement. Consider continuing the deck railing around the perimeter of the screen porch and incorporating screening into the railing structure. Or install a knee wall in the porch area of the deck and screening above. Screens that extend to floor level are subject to dents and dings. Even on a low-level deck, consider a substantial base around the screened area to protect the screening from damage.

To create a smooth visual transition between a screen porch and deck, furnish both with lightweight, mobile furnishings that coordinate or complement one another.

ABOVE: **This deck provides a private area to relax, thanks to a lattice trellis and wisteria vine, right, that shield the deck from full view while still allowing in cool breezes. The arbor shades the deck without blocking light from entering the screen porch. The sheltered porch is furnished like an outdoor room.**

OPPOSITE: **On this riverside home, a screen porch was a necessity to keep bugs at bay. The grand, two-story porch opens to an expansive multilevel deck that steps down to the lawn.**

deck to pool

Relaxing by a pool can be almost as enjoyable as being in the water. Take care in planning the area around the pool to achieve the most enjoyment from the space. As with any deck site, planning a deck near a pool means thinking about how you want to use the space. Do you envision lavish pool parties? A large deck space would accommodate the gatherings. Or do you plan to start your day in solitude by swimming in a small lap pool and then reading the day's news as you dry off? A small deck protected by privacy screens would fulfill your vision. Do you need a shady spot to rest after splashing in a sun-drenched pool? Plan an overhead structure.

Consider aesthetics as well as
function. The deck and pool designs
should complement each other and your
house. A deck and pool proportionate to
one another and to the site are the most
visually pleasing. Placing an enormous
pool adjacent to a tiny standard deck
would look odd and probably not function well.

As with any deck, landscaping is
critical. Landscaping can be a strong

unifying device between the deck, pool,
house, and yard.

**OPPOSITE TOP: Nestled just below the
pool, this small deck provides an ideal
location to rest after a swim. Landscaping
with perennials and shrubs beside the pool
and around the deck unifies the entire
space and creates a natural appearance.**

**OPPOSITE BOTTOM: Low-growing plants
hug the stone stairs that lead from a deck
made for sunbathing to a pond-like pool.**

**ABOVE: Designed for entertaining, this
multilevel deck allows plenty of space
for revelers. Multiple staircases make it
easy to access the pool, surrounded by
natural stone.**

transitions with landscaping

When planning your deck, include appropriate landscaping that helps put the finishing touches on your new outdoor space. Design foundation plantings as an attractive cover for the area underneath decks. Even if you include skirting in your deck plans, the area can look bare without greenery. Consider planting even the most basic of gardens to provide an attractive transition between your deck and the yard beyond.

Take time to look through books and magazines and to visit nurseries and garden centers for landscaping ideas, just as you took time to gather ideas for your new deck. Consult a landscape architect or landscape designer for ideas or for a complete landscape plan. You also can request a complete landscape plan as part of your deck plans. The landscaping is an enduring part of your outdoor space. Thoughtful planning should provide a landscape that offers years of enjoyment and satisfaction.

ASSESSING LANDSCAPING NEEDS

When developing a landscape plan that works for you, it is critical to assess what is needed to attractively transition your new deck to the surrounding area. If you have a deck built off the ground—even by just a few feet—foundation plantings should fill in the bare area under the deck and soften the lines between the deck and the yard.

Think about how you access the yard from your deck. Note the mature sizes of plants you are considering planting around the deck: Plants grown to full size may block access or views. Perennials may not reach full size for a couple of growing seasons;

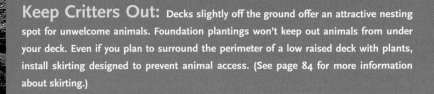

Keep Critters Out: Decks slightly off the ground offer an attractive nesting spot for unwelcome animals. Foundation plantings won't keep out animals from under your deck. Even if you plan to surround the perimeter of a low raised deck with plants, install skirting designed to prevent animal access. (See page 84 for more information about skirting.)

slow-growing shrubs and trees can take years to mature.

Look at the plans for your new deck. Note how the structure affects your current landscaping. Foundation shrubs along your home and surrounding gardens may be removed to make way for the deck, leaving bare dirt around it. Compensate for these changes in the landscape plan.

Remember that landscaping includes more than plants, shrubs, and trees. Consider other hardscapes, such as walks, paths, fences, walls, and patios, besides the deck itself. A deck could step down to a patio, for example. Or if steps lead from the deck to the yard, the landing might offer an opportunity for a flagstone path to replace an existing expanse of grass. Just as you selected deck materials and finishes that complement or blend with your home, plan to use hardscape materials that harmonize with both.

Landscaping elements create the ideal environment for a new deck. If the neighbors have a clear view onto the deck you envision as a private retreat, design a wall of tall evergreens to block the view and shelter your space.

ASSESSING YOUR STYLE

Style is another important consideration when defining your landscaping plans. The architecture and color scheme of your home, your personal tastes, experience with plants and gardening, and

OPPOSITE: Even low-level decks benefit from plants along the perimeter. Here blooming potted plants on the deck partner with flower gardens to create a colorful border.

BELOW: Soften the edges of a platform deck with curved edges and soft plants that spread gently over the edge of the deck.

lifestyle should all influence your choices. Consider the style of your home and deck. A charming cottage and diminutive deck would be better complemented by an informal garden featuring long-blooming flowers rather than formal clipped hedges. Look at the color combinations used on the exterior of your home. Purple and fuchsia blooms may look jarring against red brick.

Personal taste is important. Spend time strolling your neighborhood, noting the varieties, shapes, and colors of trees, shrubs, flowers, and grasses that you like and that would look striking with your style of home. Take into account your lifestyle as you plan land-scaping. If your lifestyle is extremely busy and you want to spend your few precious moments at home with your feet propped up enjoying a glass of cool lemonade on the deck, select low-care shrubs and trees to add to the landscape.

FOUNDATION PLANTINGS

Foundation plantings are shrubs and other plants positioned near the base of a structure—often a house or porch—to conceal the otherwise bare foundation. Foundation plantings are ideal around the perimeter of a deck. They create a pleasing transition between the deck and surrounding landscape, as well as shield the area under a raised deck. The most attractive foundation plantings are care-fully designed to progress from the tallest part of the deck down to the lawn or groundcover. Foundation plantings shouldn't be limited to one solid row of evergreen shrubs. A single row or hedge of shrubs lined up along the perimeter of the deck separates the structure from the rest of the landscape instead of tying the two together.

Incorporate variety. Successful foundation plantings include a variety of colors, shapes, and textures that coordi-nate with the home, deck, and adjacent gardens. But avoid planting one of every-thing you like. Instead, group similar plants for maximum impact.

Consider shape. Look at the plant tag for the natural shape of the plant. If you want a formal look, don't select informal plants with graceful, arching branches and expect to prune them into a compact globe. Select a more compact, geometrically shaped shrub.

Pay attention to size. One common mistake is to underestimate the mature size of a plant and select plants that quickly crowd a deck and block views or access. Don't assume you can prune a plant to maintain the size you desire. Though some plants are ideal for heavy shearing, others will soon look unattractive or unwieldy despite your efforts. Provide enough room for plants to spread. Use mature size information on the plant tag to correctly position plants in relation to your deck and to one another. Understand that when you initially plant the new landscape, flowers and shrubs will look too small for the spacing. Be patient; they will be ideal after a few seasons.

Plant in layers. Position the tallest layer of shrubs or small, ornamental trees nearest the deck. In front of the tallest layer, plant perennials and medium-height dwarf varieties of shrubs. The outermost layer should consist of groundcover or short perennials. Fill in with annuals to provide instant seasonal color. Three-layer foundation plantings require beds about 6 to 10 feet wide, depending on the specific plants you choose.

ON THE DECK

When space is available, use the deck as a stage to feature containers and hanging baskets of flowers. Coordinate the colors of foliage and flowers and their containers with the palette of fabrics and furnishings on your deck. Or pick colors and varieties from the surrounding landscape to better integrate the deck and gardens. In any case, fragrant plants are ideal for deck containers.

Plant Selection: The most successful landscape plans for decks take into account the conditions of the site. Pay attention to the exposure of the area and choose plants with matching light requirements. Southern exposure with no shade, for example, may dry out soil more quickly than in other areas. In such a location choose plants that prefer it dry, or plan to water frequently.

OPPOSITE: **Plan for an overall landscape scheme.** Landscaping for this deck and spa maintains a formal yet relaxed theme thanks to a manicured hedge and repeated white pergolas on the deck and at the back of the yard. Tall shrubs and full trees along the perimeter of the property provide privacy on the deck and in the yard.

ABOVE: **Tiered plant heights effectively transition between a raised deck and the lawn.** Colorful foliage adds interest to the area around this deck, even when the flower bed is not in peak bloom. Mulch helps control weeds and maintains moisture. Brick edging prevents grass from encroaching on the garden.

This deck, patio, and garden combination does what every deck-based landscape plan should aspire to—link home to garden and front yard to back, while artfully blurring the lines between indoors and out.

A duo of sun-drenched decks for cooking everyday meals and entertaining serve as an extension of the home's architecture. The decks fill in a sloping grade, stepping down to a tree-shaded patio ensconced in greenery. Screening unwanted views and softening the landscape's geometry, artful shrubbery and kaleidoscopic blooms spill from beds, window boxes, and containers.

The pair of decks supply contemporary convenience, vintage character, and seclusion. Because of a grade change between the front yard and back, the decks are terraced down to the patio. This provides room for a cooking area near the kitchen on the upper level, with plenty of seating and eating space for privacy tucked down on the lower deck.

The backyard decks blend with the period detailing of the remodeled Victorian farmhouse. The skirting is custom-built from 1-inch-square lattice, the railings exude porch-like appeal, and the home's interior columns echo the design of the substantial paneled posts capped by sculptural finials.

All of the deck framework, rails, posts, lattice, and stair risers are crafted from cedar and painted white to match the trim on the home. To further boost the inside-out appeal, the decking and stair treads are crafted from Pau Lope, a dense, knot-free Brazilian hardwood with the look of teak. When it's oiled, the decking resembles the hardwood floors inside the house.

Retaining walls of 12-inch-thick flagstone create a seamless transition from the deck to the bluestone and tumbled-brick patio and around to the side courtyard. The walls also prevent erosion, provide secure, nestled-in-the-garden seating, and

support loads of spaces for shrubs, vines, and flowers.

Although formal gardens grace the front yard, the landscape takes on a more natural feel as the gardens wrap around the side of the house. Here a meandering flagstone path leads to a vine-covered arbor, brick courtyard, and the cohesive composition of the patio and decks beyond.

ABOVE: The arbor matches the posts on the picket fence, front porch, and deck. Lattice gives vines and roses a toehold and links the structure to the decks.

RIGHT: An upper deck places the grilling area close to the kitchen, while a lower deck provides seating and eating space screened by plantings for privacy.

OPPOSITE: The decks bask in abundant sunshine, while the patio affords a shady retreat. The lower lattice panels hide air-conditioning units, support clematis, and offer a crisp white backdrop for plantings contained by flagstone retaining walls.

Stepping down gently into the sloping yard, this multilevel deck spans a 12-foot drop and turns a once unusable outdoor space into a prime area for entertaining and relaxing.

A mix of materials and multiple levels ensures that the intimate backyard retreat is anything but a staid mass of wood.

It's the embellishments that make the Western clear cedar deck a one-of-a-kind retreat. A bench system supplements the furniture and accommodates more people when entertaining. For an intricate, woven look, the benches are constructed with 2×2 strips of cedar. Two L-shape benches are built in on the lower level. Movable benches, which can be pulled away from the railing when small children visit, rest on the high end of the deck.

The deck's location, on 6 acres of wooded wetland, called for another unusual design element. Wooden kick-off mats built into the deck in front of the doors leading to the kitchen and dining room cut down on woodland debris tracked into the house. Aesthetically, the mats break up the long, wide expanse of the deck.

Rather than nails, metals clips and exterior subfloor construction adhesive

bind the 2×6 floorboards. Although the clips can take three times longer than nails to install, they save time and effort as the deck ages. With no surface nailing, nothing penetrates the wood, so no moisture seeps into the decking. In addition, there aren't any nails to worry about when it's time to sand and refinish the deck.

Built-in planters constructed of stucco and brick tie the deck to the house and yard. Cinder blocks were mortared together and covered with stucco to match the siding on the home.

Brick caps add the final touch. The same brick is used on the shallow stairs that lead from deck to patio.

The railing provides the finishing touch. Built from chunky 6×6 posts topped with 2×8 caps, it complements the house. The same brown exterior paint used on the house trim is used on the railing, protecting better than a clear stain and creating instant harmony.

ABOVE: Built-in stucco planters tie the deck to the house and yard. Topped with brick caps, the planters hold herbs, flowers, and fruit.

LEFT: In a yard with a 12-foot drop-off on one side and a gradual slope on the other, this deck provides outdoor living space where none existed. As a purely aesthetic feature, brown painted posts serve as skirting to hide the area under the deck.

OPPOSITE: Mimicking the home's Tudor style, short stucco planters and built-in benches are positioned by a set of brick steps. The deck itself was designed to preserve existing trees that provide valuable shade.

6

furnishing with style

Today's attractive, weather-resistant fabrics and furnishings create cozy, carefree outdoor living spaces. »

>> Thanks to an ever-growing appreciation for the comforts and pleasures of outdoor rooms, today's outdoor furniture and fabrics are made to withstand Mother Nature. You'll find plenty of materials and styles compatible with your design ideas and intended use. As with indoor furnishings, think style and comfort. Now is the time to relax and take time off to enjoy your new deck.

outdoor furniture

True outdoor furniture is manufactured to resist the rigors of radical temperature fluctuations and the onslaught of moisture. Although some of these durable pieces are better suited for covered areas, such as porches or gazebos, many deck products now are made to withstand direct exposure to the elements.

Arrange furniture for your deck just as you would any room. Create groupings for various activities. Place seating close enough for easy conversation, but not so close as to invade personal space. Allow for traffic flow easily between furniture groupings.

MATERIALS CHOICES

Certain materials are specifically designed to withstand the weather. Here are some durable options:

Aluminum furniture, either wrought or cast in molds, is ideal for capturing contemporary style on your deck. It's rustproof, lightweight, and generally more expensive than iron. Most aluminum furniture comes with tough, baked-on enamel finishes. When

shopping, look for thick, heavy-gauge alloys and smooth seams on welded joints. Less expensive versions feature hollow, tubular frames.

Cast- or wrought-iron furniture is heavy and durable yet prone to rust.

Also, it requires periodic touch-ups and repainting if exposed to the elements. Iron pieces are available in many styles, but the material recalls the graceful, ornate Victorian style of the late 1800s. This type of outdoor furniture is

appropriate in windy climates, where its considerable weight makes it less prone to being shifted around by gusts.

Plastic and resin furniture is inexpensive and offered in a limited choice of styles and colors. However, a low-cost set of stacking plastic chairs adds flexibility for entertaining. When buying plastic furniture, look for quality—top-grade plastic furniture has a 10-year warranty. Some plastic furniture is made from recycled materials. It is thick, heavy, and looks like wood, but never needs to be painted.

Synthetic wicker typically is made from moisture-proof polyester resins and rustproof aluminum framing. Colors mimic those of natural wicker, but they can be placed outdoors and exposed to the elements without damage. Synthetic wicker is slightly more expensive than comparable pieces made of natural wicker.

Twig furniture is usually constructed from green willow branches that are bent into sweeping curves and curlicues to form the arms, legs, and backs of the pieces. The frames are weather-resistant, but keep twig furniture sheltered to prolong its life. Exposure to direct sun may cause shrinking of the branches, which tends to loosen fasteners. Twig furniture has a carefree, rustic appeal that works well with pillows in bold colors and patterns. It is often produced locally—look for good prices at area crafts shops, farmer's markets, and roadside stands.

ABOVE: **Besides being durable and easy to maintain, resin and plastic offer style at an affordable price. The newest crop of products sport chic contemporary lines and bold colors—like these yellow and orange resin chairs paired with a blue stool.**

OPPOSITE: **With their colorful fabric seats, these canvas loungers are a portable way to brighten up any outdoor space.**

Wicker furniture has long been synonymous with gracious outdoor style. Elegantly shaped and comfortably familiar, wicker has been popular in outdoor living areas for more than a century. Natural wicker is produced in warm browns or stained with accent colors, traditionally, black or green. Natural wicker may be unfinished or sealed with marine varnish. Painted wicker is usually white. Wicker furniture should not be exposed to the elements. It should only be used under a sheltering roof and brought indoors for storage before cold weather sets in.

Wood furniture made of teak, redwood, and cypress is weather- and rot-resistant and does not require paints, stains, or other protective coatings. Left to age naturally, these handsome pieces mellow into a silvery gray within a year. They can be left plain or spruced up with mildew-resistant cushions and pillows. Look for brands made from woods harvested on tree farms that are systematically replanted. Pieces made from average-quality, furniture-grade woods, such as pine, fir, and oak, need to be updated yearly with fresh coats of stain, paint, or sealer. Oil-base paints are tougher than latex. Gloss finishes last longer than semigloss or flat finishes.

ALFRESCO DINING

Decks have long provided the ideal spots for casual dinners. Increasingly, decks are host to lavish dinner parties, as well as intimate formal meals suited to sophisticated dinnerware, table linens, and candlelight. Before purchasing a table and chairs, analyze your needs. For large-scale entertaining, consider a table that comfortably seats six to eight or more, and perhaps several smaller tables for setting refreshments. If intimate dining is your style, select a smaller table.

When choosing linens and table settings for outdoor entertaining, again look to intended use for guidance. If you're planning casual family picnics, keep table decorations simple and durable—think sturdy tablecloths in stain-resistant fabrics. Or select a glass-top outdoor table that only requires a quick wipe-down after meals. For more formal dining affairs, enhance your tabletop with linens, dinnerware, stemware, and centerpieces, just as you would indoors. It can all be brought inside for safekeeping after the meal.

furniture sizing

36-INCH ROUND TABLE AND FOUR CHAIRS. Minimum Square Footage Required: A square or circle 9 feet across, a total of 80 to 90 square feet. **Ideal Square Footage for Comfort:** A square or circle 12 feet across, a total of 140 to 150 square feet.

48-INCH ROUND TABLE AND SIX CHAIRS. Minimum Square Footage Required: A square or circle 10 feet across, a total of 100 to 110 square feet. **Ideal Square Footage for Comfort:** A square or circle 13 feet across, a total of 160–180 square feet.

ADIRONDACK CHAIR. Minimum Square Footage Required: A rectangle 6 feet long and 3¹/₂ feet wide, a total of 21 square feet. **Ideal Square Footage for Comfort:** A rectangle 8 feet long and 4 feet wide, a total of 32 square feet.

BARBECUE GRILL, 18-INCH DIAMETER KETTLE TYPE. Minimum Square Footage Required: 1-foot clearance at sides and back, 3-foot clearance in front, a total of 20 square feet. **Ideal Square Footage for Comfort:** 2-foot clearance at sides and back, 4-foot clearance in front, a total of 42 square feet.

BARBECUE GRILL ON 2×3-FOOT ROLLING CART. Minimum Square Footage Required: 1-foot clearance at sides and back, 3-foot clearance in front, a total of 30 square feet. **Ideal Square Footage for Comfort:** 2-foot clearance at sides and back, 4-foot clearance in front, a total of 56 square feet.

FREESTANDING HAMMOCK WITH SELF-SUPPORTING STAND. Minimum Square Footage Required: A rectangle 9 feet long and 6 feet wide, a total of 54 square feet. **Ideal Square Footage for Comfort:** A rectangle 9 feet long and 6 feet wide, 3 feet at each side for clearance, a total of 108 square feet.

BUILT-IN BENCH SEAT 6 FEET LONG. Minimum Square Footage Required: 6 feet wide, 1¹/₂-foot wide seat, 3-foot clearance in front of seat, a total of 27 square feet. **Ideal Square Footage for Comfort:** 5-foot clearance in front of seat, a total of 39 square feet.

ABOVE: Fire-engine-red vintage chairs in a circular arrangement carve out a casual living room on a deck. A tree-stump table serves as the focal point of the outdoor area.

RIGHT: With vistas of the treetops and mountains beyond, this deck is ideal for family dining. A natural wood table set with colorful dishes and matching chairs decorated with playful pillows make for a fun, comfortable outdoor meal.

fabrics

Today's weather-resistant materials provide great outdoor style. Some synthetic fabrics faithfully reproduce the look and feel of natural fibers, such as canvas, and resist mold, mildew, and fading. Use them for cushions, pillows, and curtains to brighten and energize outdoor rooms. Fabrics may enhance privacy and protect you from the sun when they are used as canopies, curtains, or privacy screens. You can use finer fabrics on pillows and cushions, but bring them indoors when not in use.

CHOOSING FABRICS

Fabric is an ideal way to splash your deck with color. Fabrics used outdoors often feature bolder colors and larger patterns than those used indoors.

Look for fabrics that breathe and wick off water to avoid mildew. Depending on sun exposure, fade-resistant materials could be quite important. Natural fabrics are least resistant to mold and mildew, so synthetics are best for decks. Even though an upholstery fabric may be designed to repel moisture, the padding within the fabric probably is not; store padded cushions indoors when not in use.

Solution-dyed acrylics dry quickly, resist mildew and fading, and are easily sewn into soft furnishings, pillows, and curtains. Look for products that are coated with a moisture- and stain-resistant finish for improved wear.

Woven polyester is coated with vinyl to produce an especially strong, durable fabric ideal for umbrellas, hammocks, and seat cushions.

Laminated cotton is made by coating cotton fabric with acrylic or polyurethane. The result is a tough, flexible outdoor material that resists moisture. However, the natural cotton fibers are still prone to fading and mildew spotting; limit their use to sheltered areas. You can waterproof your

own fabrics with iron-on vinyl available at fabric stores.

Hearty natural fabrics such as canvas, duck, and twill are strong but only mildly resist fading. They can be used for cushions, curtains, shades, and slipcovers, but they are prone to mildew—make sure they can be removed easily for cleaning.

OPPOSITE: Fabric provides the privacy of a wall without the permanence. When it's time to be sheltered from the bright sun, a breeze, or the neighbors' eyes, this weatherproof awning-stripe panel is unfurled and tied to the porch post. The fabric rolls up like a window shade when it's time to return the room to its open-air status. A similarly patterned chair pad covers the chair seat.

ABOVE: Because of their versatility, striped outdoor fabrics are the most popular for cushions, chairs, and loungers. Classic yet informal, stripes work well with traditional, contemporary, or country styles.

BELOW: Wicker furniture and floral prints combine with a wisteria-covered arbor to create a romantic theme in this outdoor dining space. Because an open-air arbor doesn't protect against rain or wind, the table's white skirt and perhaps even the settees' upholstered cushions must be taken indoors when not in use.

accessories

Well-dressed outdoor living areas include art and accessories. Even small decorative accents imbue an outdoor space with distinctive personality and distinguish a stylish area from a generic deck.

Use your home's exterior walls to display art outdoors, especially under the eaves of the house, which provide semi-protected backdrops for weather-resistant pieces. If your deck area has no walls, use sculpture to define the space and increase its character. Or sprinkle accessories such as bird baths, potted plants, and colorful watering cans through the area.

Overhead structures offer another opportunity for accessorizing your space. Hang potted plants, lanterns, and even chandeliers from a pergola or sturdy tree branches. Open large, colorful umbrellas over dining areas.

Rugs offer splashes of color and soften the look and feel of an outdoor room. Just as with indoor spaces, outdoor area rugs anchor furniture groupings on a deck. Use rugs crafted from synthetic mildew-resistant fibers to create the coziness of an indoor room outside. When the rugs become soiled, spray off dirt with a hose.

RIGHT: **An elegant outdoor room displays unexpected charm with the addition of a striking chandelier affixed to an overhead structure.**

OPPOSITE TOP: **Dangling from galvanized chain, three windows form a floating wall at the side of a deck. Flowered valances on the windows, pillows on the built-in benches, and lamps and candles attached to a pergola's posts enhance the space.**

OPPOSITE BOTTOM: **A mirror affixed to an exterior house wall reflects green foliage beyond the deck. Painted wicker furniture, yellow pillows, and freshly cut flowers create the feeling of an indoor room.**

cost planning

Before building your dream deck, determine if the project fits within your budget and covers the essentials. »

>> Deck projects are as unique as the people who build them. Even so, different projects have common features, such as size, level of complexity, and amenities that make them useful for approximating costs. In this chapter you'll find illustrations of six deck projects—small, medium, and large deck sizes, each with two levels of features: basic and upgraded.

small deck

A small deck, such as this one, provides an ideal locale for quiet at-home escapes—a spot to relax with a good book or to enjoy the beauty of a backyard garden. If a place for restful solitude is the goal for your deck, a small deck may provide all the space you need. Of course, small decks are ideal if you have limited outdoor space and want to maximize outdoor use. Modest-size decks are also appropriate with a bungalow that would be overwhelmed by an expansive deck.

This 10×12-foot platform deck is positioned only 12 inches above the ground, offering an easy transition from house to yard and requiring no railings. Steps ease the transition from house to deck and deck to yard.

BASIC
• Decking: pressure-treated lumber
Materials: $722.28
Approximate contractor's bid, including labor and materials: $3,066.15

UPGRADE
• Decking: ipe, double-diagonal pattern
• Built-in benches
• Trellis behind bench on far side of deck, or arbor in same position
Materials: $2,711.51
Approximate contractor's bid, including labor and materials: $7,894.59

What Will It Cost? The vignettes provided in this chapter include a few details of construction and approximate costs for materials—as well as estimates of the cost of having a professional contractor complete the job. These figures, provided by Archadeck, America's largest deck builder, reflect North American averages. You should expect to pay more for materials and labor in more distant locations, such as Hawaii, and lower costs in a less remote locale, where costs of transporting materials are lower. Use these project estimates to ballpark the cost of your own deck. Once planning is underway, get firm estimates from professionals so your project plans and your budget closely agree.

UPGRADE OPTIONS

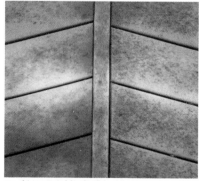
Decking: Double-diagonal pattern

Decking: Ipe

Trellis: Supports flowering vines and provides privacy

Built-in Benches

Basic Small-Size Deck

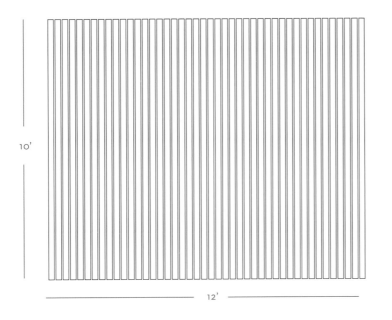

10'

12'

Upgraded Small-Size Deck

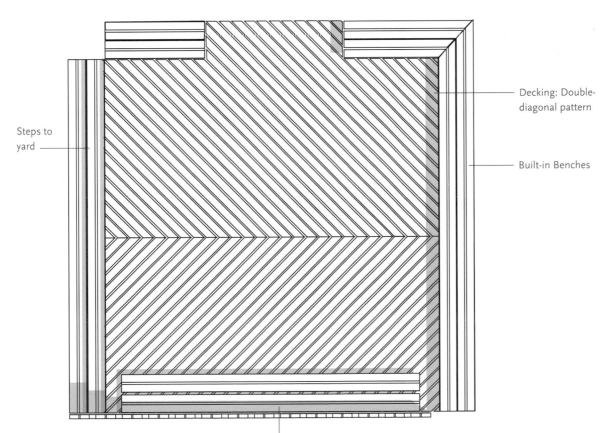

Steps to yard

Decking: Double-diagonal pattern

Built-in Benches

Trellis: Positioned behind bench to attractively screen unwanted views and to support flowering vine.

medium deck

A medium-size deck, such as this one, creates an outdoor room. At approximately 20×15 feet, the deck provides space for alfresco dining just outside the kitchen, with additional space for a small gathering or family activities. A deck of this size integrates better with most story-and-a-half and two-story homes than a typical tiny builder's deck, and it offers ample room for activities.

The raised deck offers the opportunity for enclosed under-deck storage. For locations with a view, alternative railing styles, such as stainless-steel cabling or safety glass, preserve the view in all directions.

BASIC

- Decking: pressure-treated lumber; boards parallel to house
- No skirting; river rock or gravel underneath deck
- Standard, most basic railing style around deck
- No overhead structures

Materials: $2,361.33

Approximate contractor's bid, including labor and materials: $7,516.12

UPGRADE

- Decking: cedar; diagonal pattern
- Overhead structure similar to illustration, or flat-top pergola over portion of deck, with overhead in illustration
- Skirting around deck, with one part that opens on hinge for storage
- Metal wire railing, perhaps stainless-steel cabling
- Built-in storage bench next to house, under window on left; doubles as seating bench

Materials = $8,729.76

Approximate contractor's bid, including labor and materials = $23,647.52

UPGRADE OPTIONS

Railing: Stainless-steel cabling

Decking: Cedar; diagonal pattern

Overhead Structure: Provides shade for portion of deck

Storage Bench: Doubles as additional seating

Lattice Skirting: Attractive under-deck coverage; hinges allow access to handy storage area

Basic Medium-Size Deck

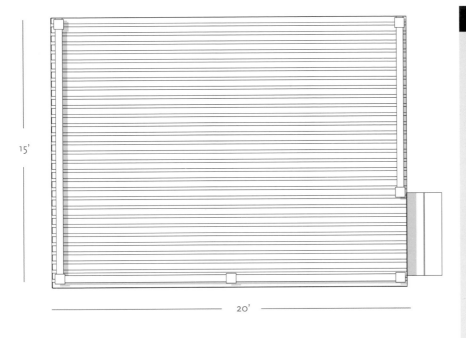

15'

20'

Upgraded Medium-Size Deck

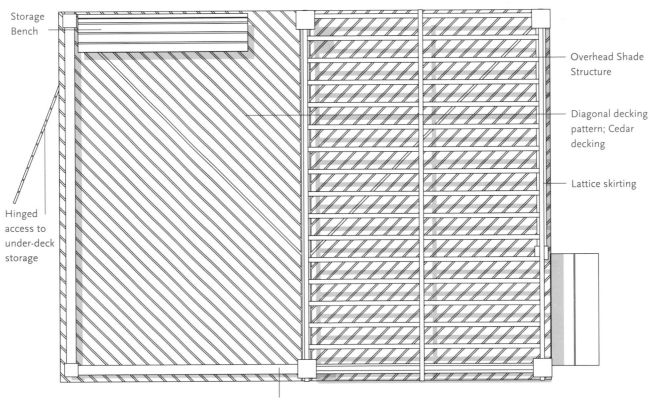

Storage Bench

Overhead Shade Structure

Diagonal decking pattern; Cedar decking

Lattice skirting

Hinged access to under-deck storage

Stainless-steel cable railings

large deck

A large deck should be designed as a multifunctional area, with space for a variety of outdoor activities. At approximately 650 square feet, this large, multilevel deck project adds an abundance of outdoor living area and smoothly integrates with a number of entry points to the back of a house.

A key benefit of this deck is access. Doors open to the deck from the kitchen at one end of the house and from a master bedroom on the other. The deck also transitions well to the yard. Platforms gradually step down from the highest level of the deck nearest the house to the lowest platform that opens to the yard.

Another successful design element is the use of individual spaces—some designated by a shift in level, others by decking patterns—to give each area of the deck personality and to indicate rooms. The octagon, for example, is a natural location for outdoor meals—particularly when sheltered by a screened gazebo, as in the upgrade. The space adjacent to the master bedroom is a natural spot for intimate conversations and relaxing at day's end. Open areas nearer the kitchen and family room offer plenty of space for large gatherings.

BASIC
• Decking: pressure-treated lumber, boards parallel to house
• Basic railing
Materials: $4,320.49
Approximate contractor's bid, including labor and materials: $15,650.66

UPGRADE
• Decking: composite, with patterns changing on each area of the deck to visually distinguish various areas
• Gazebo on octagon portion of deck
• Built-in spa
• Privacy screen to shelter spa
• Outdoor kitchen with large built-in grill, prep sink, and counter space with storage under counter
• Built-in seating along perimeter of deck, with planters along top of back portion of seats
• Wide stairs with easy access to lawn
• Skirting around perimeter
Materials: $21,855.26
Approximate contractor's bid, including labor and materials: $46,679.47

Considerations

Because of their size, large decks offer the chance to include the most amenities and options. Don't simply add as much deck space or as many amenities as you can afford, however. A huge deck may overwhelm your house, and you may not need every possible amenity. Though this deck is loaded with special features, each contributes to a carefully planned outdoor living space.

Here are other amenities to consider for a large deck:
• Pergola or arbor for filtered shade
• Hinged access to under-deck storage
• Custom railings
• Hinged storage benches that double as extra seating

UPGRADE OPTIONS

Wide Stairs for Easy Access to the Yard

Built-in Seating and Planters

Screened Gazebo

Built-in Spa with Privacy Screen

Basic Large-Size Deck

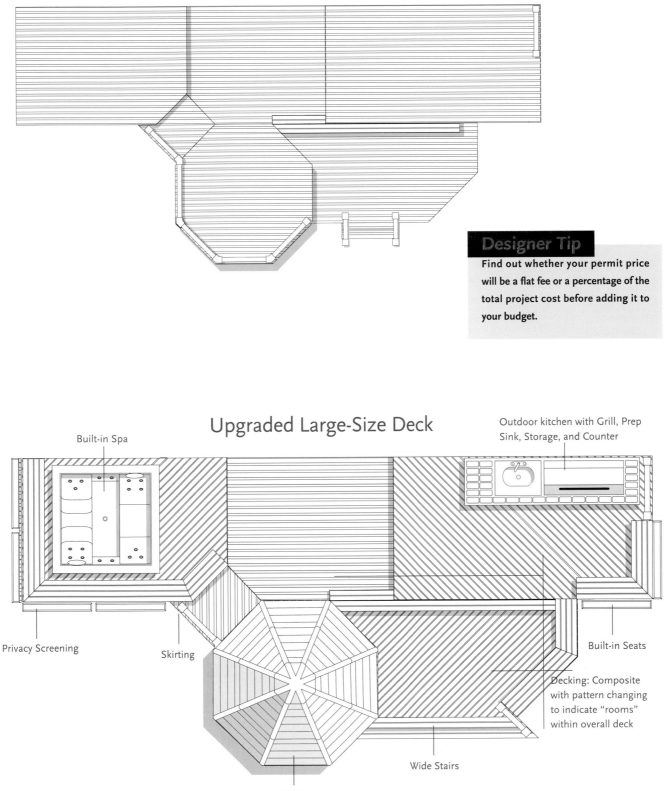

Designer Tip

Find out whether your permit price will be a flat fee or a percentage of the total project cost before adding it to your budget.

Upgraded Large-Size Deck

Built-in Spa

Outdoor kitchen with Grill, Prep Sink, Storage, and Counter

Privacy Screening

Skirting

Built-in Seats

Decking: Composite with pattern changing to indicate "rooms" within overall deck

Gazebo

Wide Stairs

final deck checklist

Spare yourself some hassle and headache, as well as last-minute budget busters, by checking this list of deck-project essentials. Though it won't cover everything needed for special upgrades, such as a fireplace or full outdoor kitchen, checking your plans against these points should keep your project on the right track.

PLANNING:

• Does the deck comply with area building codes?
• Is there plenty of space for planned outdoor activities?
• Is there enough space for amenities and furnishings, such as tables and chairs, and for the people who will use them?
• Will traffic flow easily between the house and the deck?
• Is it easy to access the yard from the deck?
• Are individual spaces for specific uses designated on a large deck?
• Will the deck visually integrate with the house?
• Will at least a portion of the deck be shaded, if desired, during peak use times?
• If privacy is a concern, are privacy screens planned?
• Does the deck contain storage elements, such as built-ins or access doors?
• Do you have detailed plans of the final deck design?
• If you plan to work with contractors, builders, and other professionals, have you reviewed and signed contracts specifying all work, materials, and responsibilities?

COMPONENTS:

• Does your project list include all project components that follow?

• Have you budgeted for all the project components listed below?

MATERIALS
Lumber:
• Substructure (ledgers, joists, posts, beams)
• Railings (rail posts, balusters, top rails)
• Stairway parts (stringers, risers, treads)
• Decking

Fasteners:
• Post anchors
• Joist hangers
• Bolts
• Screws
• Nails

Finishes:
• Stain
• Sealer
• Paint

Other materials:
• Alternate materials planned for decking and railings

• Skirting
• Fill for under deck, such as weed-blocking landscape fabric and river rock

LABOR
• Site clearing and prep
• Digging footings
• Pouring footings
• Constructing substructure
• Installing decking
• Building stairs (if needed)
• Installing railings (if needed)
• Finishing deck

SPECIAL FEATURES
• Do the final deck plans account for any special features, such as an outdoor kitchen, spa, or gazebo?
• Will structural elements adequately support heavy features, such as a spa?
• If plans include adding a special feature later, will proper prep work—such as roughing in utilities—be done during initial construction prep work?

DIY considerations

Building a deck is a common do-it-your-self project, primarily for good reasons. Even weekend carpenters can construct a deck suitable for years of outdoor fun. That doesn't mean, however, that it's wise for everyone to tackle deck planning and construction without the involvement of a pro. Here are some considerations to make before undertaking a do-it-yourself deck project.

COST

If dollar signs dancing before your eyes are the impetus for building alone, remember that there can be considerable costs incurred during a DIY project. Deck construction requires more than a hammer and nails. Though you won't need many specialized tools, if you're just starting out and don't own a circular saw, miter saw, level, square, saw horses, and the like, purchasing this equipment—or even renting it for the project—can be expensive.

You also need to consider transportation: How will you get all of the materials from the home improvement center or lumberyard to your home? If you need to rent a truck or pay for delivery, add those fees to the cost of your deck. You may pay higher prices for materials than a contractor who buys in greater volume; some contractors are willing to pass on that savings to you.

You also should factor in your time when considering cost. If your weekends are already packed with activities, and taking vacation is the only way to find time to build the deck, your time may be more valuably spent in other pursuits.

BUILDING CODES

Deck building and design professionals should be familiar with area building codes and designing and constructing decks that comply with those codes. While homeowners certainly can meet with the building department to ensure that a project is up to code, it can simplify the process to involve a pro. In addition, consider that if the deck you planned and built is inspected and not up to code, you'll be responsible for making the necessary changes to meet code.

PHYSICAL LABOR

Digging footings, mixing concrete, and filling footings is no easy task, particularly if you need to move concrete from the driveway in front of your home to the back of the house where the new deck is to be built. Attaching fasteners to secure decking for the entire surface area of the deck also is more work than you might think. Realistically assess your fitness level and the actual work involved in building a deck.

SAFETY

Though building a deck is certainly not one of the more hazardous home improvement projects, there are safety considerations. Job site safety is critical for any project, particularly if you have children or pets. Children are naturally drawn to construction sites; the saws, nails, screws, and other materials can pose hazards. If you are constructing the deck, consider where children can play and who will be available to supervise them. Where will pets be contained?

Consider also the duration of the project. Pros may be able to finish a deck in a week or so. A novice do-it-yourselfer may take numerous weekends or longer. Do you want to secure a building site for that length of time? Also

consider your personal safety. You need to be alert and cautious while operating any power tool. Make sure you have the proper safety equipment and purchase or rent quality tools with the necessary safety features.

INCONVENIENCE

Be honest with how you will handle the inconvenience of building a deck. You probably want the deck as a place to relax after work and on weekends. Do you really want to spend that potential relaxation time building the deck yourself? Unless you are already skilled at home improvement projects, it will likely take you longer than anticipated to finish the deck. Factor in weather delays, as well as unexpected trips back to the home improvement center or hardware store for additional supplies. If, on the other hand, you enjoy home improvement projects as a hobby and a way to relax, and you've taken into account all the considerations above, pull out that hammer and saw and start building the deck of your dreams.

index

Better Homes and Gardens
dream the perfect home, then make it a reality.
GREAT DECKS & OUTDOOR LIVING
Better Homes and Gardens baths Dream It. Plan It. Remodel It.
Better Homes and Gardens Additions PLANNER
Better Homes and Gardens kitchens Dream It. Plan It. Remodel It.
Better Homes and Gardens Porch & Sunroom PLANNER
Look for these great Home Improvement titles—wherever books are sold.